LETTERS *from the* COMMONS

LETTERS
from the
COMMONS

Kevin Holmes

WARD STREET PRESS · SEATTLE

Letters from the Commons
ISBN: 978-0-9844969-4-5

BOOK DESIGN BY VEE SAWYER
COVER PHOTO BY VEE SAWYER

Contents

LETTERS *from the* COMMONS

Preface

THESE ARE ESSAYS, ATTEMPTS AT THOUGHTFUL-
ness, written for my grown children, very much
as a calling after them, a wait-but-I-forgot-to-
tell-you-this wave from the porch. Maybe there
are other children grown who can find in these
some parts of the common conversation, something to speak of to each other or to children of
their own, something of ourselves among all of
the others, our relatives all, in what was and may
yet again be the commons of the living world.

Kevin Holmes
July 2012

Energy

ENERGY COMES TO OUR KNOWLEDGE OF IT AL-
ready shaped, the living and nonliving its forms
and transforms, already conveyed through the
fundamental forces we ply to our trade. Civilization is tuned to the electromagnetic fundamental,
the collective body from which we sing, particularly our extensions, our machines do, hum and
sing, a steady unflickering sine. We've funded
these extensions in electric currency, the base to
which we seek to reduce nearly everything, its
juice adding sparkle to our digital smile.

It's the expansive, explosive reactions, the rapid energy transforms we've used for mobility that
move us, harnessed to a kinetic conversion, its

contained reaction driving the transports we've crafted to carry us and our claims, across land, sea, air and space. We've oiled our passage in fossilized sunlight, ancient life earth-condensed into its hydrocarbon essence, one stage in the transformation of the living world, a stage we've aborted to a consequence beyond our scope.

Before oil was coal, fossilized layers of mud-soaked plants that soon again may be king as oil recedes into less profitable strata. Still, oil drives the machines that bore and tunnel or level the mountains, wreaking a toxic devastation for the proclaimed cost-effective coal that now smokes its clouds over China.

With unbounded energy, what couldn't we do? As part of our program of finding out, we've primed the nuclear fundamental, feeding the firebox split atoms instead of coal. Works like a charm, sort of, bouncing nuclei to do the conversion to expansive heat for the old potboiler. The side and after effects are impressive though. Once uncovered, the radioisotopes fling their weight around, life- annihilators of mythic proportion, and tenacious, measuring their swathe in geologic time.

Nothing like gravity and mass for a good ride though, once on their way. With planets out of reach, water is the only mass on earth mobile enough to scale the gravitational fundamental. Any river worth its salt has a dam or ten on it, funneling the mass to turbines spinning generators and peeling off electrons for the grid, the now ubiquitous kinetic to electromagnetic conversion. Give a river a dam and it'll twirl your turbines till the well runs dry.

'Course life is the preeminent energy transformer. Despite the hubris of the empirical civilizers, there's nothing of the created world that can approach its totaled efficiencies, its full cycle. We know this, or at least are beginning to, which is why we're so focused on biotech and nanotech, closer approximations to the living world. Biotech attempts its extensions of the created world by reconfiguring and reshaping existing forms of living energy, as well as creating new, synthesized forms: generating biomass to feed the furnaces, biofuel to feed the transports. Captive organisms, engineered and not, to produce either or both by harvesting their monocultures from vast terrestrial or marine plantations. The nanotech extension too attempts to reconfigure and reshape existing forms of energy, as well as new forms, though in contrast to biotech, in shapes that we recognize only as nonliving matter, the materials of energy conversion and storage.

If the laws of thermodynamics are to be believed, there's no such thing as free energy. All transformations have a price, and if neither energy nor matter can be created or destroyed, the price is always exacted. The living world is a dynamic web of relationships and emergent properties arising from these relationships, generating new relationships that further extend and reconfigure already massively complex feedback loops. From this living web to which we belong is the price exacted.

Nor can we replace our existing energy habit with so-called clean, renewable energy. The living world doesn't scale to our purpose, only its own, which encompasses our needs, but immeasurably more. The renewable energy that is possible, is so only in a local context. We can capture and use energy from the waste streams of the living world, as long as we ensure that any waste we produce is immediately available to the living world. We can capture and use energy from the growth of the living world, as long as we simultaneously protect and care for all of its sustaining relationships. Yet the local does not scale to a civilization such as ours, modeled on immobilized, centralized, captive energy transformers, scaling production to a profit unrecognized in the living world. There is no renewable energy for such a misfit, nothing even close, only further advertising parodies.

Forms of energy that won't do a full day's work don't enter into our accounting, having no value worth valuing, no profit we recognize. On civilization's scales there isn't much, if anything, that can balance a profitable energy source. How much life does it take to equal that weight?

Do you see them, most beloved, the true aliens? They're holding hostage all our relatives. They're holding hostage our children, our children's children. Do you see them yet? They move under any flag. They've captured the conversation. The only subject is ransom, what we'll pay, what the entire living world will pay.

Power

IN THE ABSENCE OF ANY CONSTRAINT, WE'D BE immortal, the gift we once gave to gods, our highest exemplars, since attempting to give it to ourselves was so conspicuously unsuccessful. Perhaps, after all, we have or had gods solely to receive what we value most, to keep it safe, and embody what in the flux of the living world we could not. And perhaps calling them gods is distinctly less applicable now, having achieved some degree of familiarity. We find little need to distinguish the mythos of our time, believing a mythos to be an historical artifact, supplanted by empirical reality. Our mythos isn't apparent to us, yet it's among us, here in our common ground, reflected in all that we are and would be, all that we believe: in our presumptions, our premises, in the entire human-created world. It's part of the continuum we've carried and has carried us through millennia, that remains with us forming and reforming in our image, and it's where we define power.

Energy is the universal fundamental. On this basis, the living world exists only in as much as it successfully transforms energy. When the processes used to transform energy are thwarted or become dysfunctional, the living world improves its processes, finds new ones, begins to disappear, or does all of these things, perhaps at once. Although we've attempted in every way imaginable to assert the independence of our created world, to extend what we've created as far as possible from its living progenitor, the most we've been able to do is disparage and ignore the relationships.

The created world is of the living world, fully engaged in its process of transforming energy. There is no aspect of the created world for which this is not so. Whether cathedrals or catechisms, instruments or music, machines or algorithms, satellites or communication, missiles or malignance, all things material or immaterial, word, thought or deed, all are participating in the transforming process that makes and maintains the living world. This is written everywhere, inscribed in our genetics, in our physics, our chemistry, in our libraries, from Sophocles to Einstein. Solely because we are still here, all that we have ever known, ever been or done has transformed with us. The mythos has transformed with us.

Of the gifts that we have given in creating the mythos, the greatest of our gifts, because we esteemed it so, was immortality, perpetual life, or as we'd now describe it, the ability to control the transformation of energy. By every lens we have, physics, chemistry, philosophy, this is our definition of power. And this above all others, is the aspect of the mythos that civilization, ours and many before it, has embodied: an unremitting need to harness energy's transformation, to manifest the gift we gave, immortal power.

That we are impelled to acquire and consume energy sources in any form is not an aberration, not the madness it might seem. The impulse is not driven by any market, only the variance of its sources. In the hand of power, the aspect of the mythos that is power, the living world exists to transform energy only for our consumption, an appetite that increases in proportion to our creation, civilization's growth, the extension of the created world. Power is its measure and our desire.

It's necessary to know a thing to alter it. If we would change the course of power, most beloved, we need to know how and from where it arises in us. We need to see clearly its face. Only then can we take back the gift that after all, is a gift of power only because we make it so. Only because we have honored this gift beyond the life that we are, beyond the living world itself.

Earth

We walked out of Africa across the broad expressive face of the earth, terra: the ground upon which we become ourselves and to which we return to others. That to which we arrive, claim, and from which we depart. That which sustains and nourishes, holds all we have ever been or will be. That to which we reduce all unwanted. This, our common ancestry, smudges whitewashed futures, the dust of ours and others passing, carried in the wind that carries our breath. We've no word formed without it and none that is its compass. We've walked out upon its face and sought direction, from terra itself, from all our relatives, those others we choose to find beneath us; listening finally, only to ourselves, extended upon conceptions immaculately our own, our voices echoing down glistening empirical halls, and somewhere, from somewhere, there passes or intrudes into our talk, another vastly older, immeasurably larger conversation among the ancients, the elemental progenitors.

The biogeochemical cycles, the conversation among the elements in which we and all our relatives are messenger and message, expression and gesture, have changed, accommodating the terraforming that is our civilization's wake. The living soil, the shallow surface upon which depend the carbon, nitrogen and oxygen cycles and all terrestrial life, the living energy transformers, is gravely weakened, its strength depleting under our hand. It has sustained us for millennia because it in turn was being sustained, a principle and process of mutuality we do not practice, because we think we no longer live there. We entomb our bodies to ensure it will be as long as possible before we die there either.

The living soil is to us a producer, no different than any other in this respect, and one that we find inefficient to our purposes. We've spent over a century attempting to improve agricultural production, using the finest empirical science available, and have succeeded. We've succeeded as well in exhausting and destroying the living soil at a consummate rate, but the life of the soil was not, nor is it yet, our measure. Having depleted most of the available ancient stores of energy, the fossil fuels, we figure that ubiquitous biomass may be the new contender for our energy love. And if we can't get increased production out of the soil, the plan is to bioengineer our way around it, making plants that'll thrive on less.

Those folks among us who have spent lifetimes, their own and their elders, attending to the elemental conversation, are few. They've a language that has grown, that grows, from their participation in that ancient conversation. They've survived a centuries long concerted attack from a civilization to which they are anathema. They're the thread by which we hang, though nearly every human agency on earth will dispute this, will tell you in a promising, consoling language that grows more strident at your approach, to ignore, forget these useless atavists, this unfortunate detritus left in the wake of progress. Old and young, they're still here, beleaguered, mistrustful of those without the language, the heart, the horizon of their care.

You'll find them at the interstice, most beloved, the opening, the place in which we first found ourselves, the place we've painted on cavern walls and every surface imaginable; in the clay we've held and molded in grace and figure, hewn opulent in stone, where the ebb and flow meet full and ready: the parting of the ways.

Air

IT'S EVERYWHERE, AIR, GETS IN, ON, AMONG, IN-side everything, and doesn't come out in the wash. It is the wash. A paradoxical being, both transient and abiding, its constitution changes as it circuits, in accord with others, with what's needed now and next, its ebb and flow exhausting and invigorating. We're part of its filter and pump, drawing and pulsing to a cyclic axis we can only guess at, lending our leverage to the gravitational swing.

We speak air, burbling it into phonemes for our humansong. Stopped, nasalized, affricated or fricatived to an interval. Out-flung aspirations, spoken always on the wing. Its atmosphere regained, the air goes off tinged by our song-spun breath of it. What is its measure to the cycle, this speechified contribution of ours? Nature offers no fruitless interface, nothing that does not in turn contribute its own metabolized push or pull, nothing that does not put shoulder to the wheel. What does our sonance impart to the gathering? Does our speech pearl molecules to one of the cycles, as do algae in upholding the sulphured foundations through DMSP exhalations? We have questions for you, air.

Thought has, perhaps is, air. What distinction can we presume? There is no biochemical or electromagnetic medium that is air's fundament, that precedes its shaping. No message carried in its absence. Its composition influences, induces or impedes the act, the notion, the presumption of thought. Does a tremor accompany thought as it does speech, an undulation of the common air?

The elemental air is for us oxygen, and though we fancy carbon, if possession is nine-tenths of a thing, we have it in oxygen, drawn from the H2O of our own transported seas. There you have it, oxygen life forms thcn; legged terrestrial balloons, we confess.

Most earthly life is grown thereby, a reciprocal care and feeding performance played for charity, a perennial Living World Benefit where all share the stage. The reviews, though, have taken an unfavorable turn these past few centuries.

It's the preeminent medium for thermal transforms. Heat energy moves equably and efficiently into the living world on air's wings. The sun's release, current or stored and ancient, shares this same breath with us all. Shall we gather ourselves to moment this most common of all our relationships, and hold this air, this breath, dear? Does air remember us?

It goes around, with or without our help, most beloved. Maybe it's the lack of genuflection that explains our indifference to air's well-being, or conversely, its omnipresence suggesting our own impotence. We can hold it only for a metabolic moment, for a bit of biochemical conversation before it's out the door, hailed by any number of our relatives needing a word.

Water

WE'RE TERRESTRIAL CARRIERS, GIVEN OUR MEA-
sure from seas beyond telling, these same seas filling the wombs of our birth, our bodies coloring
its salted blood to the spectrum available to our
eyes. We ferry overland in cytoplasmic trunks, this
our contribution of metabolic life-trust, to purposes forgotten beyond what profit we can recognize.
We're our own harbor, afloat in our own bays and
estuaries, subject as all others to the tidal impera-
tives that sluice through us, the water we need and
that which we need no longer. We think it ours,
this aqueous body, sharing immensely more than
it can contain, containing only by variance subtle

and permeate, our course continually diffuse, the boundaries holding long enough for our assurances, the plots and models that are our comfort, persisted only by relationships that constantly inundate all. Is this water ours?

Water moves the living world, the elements, minerals of the carriers carried, moving uniquely in the universe apparently, perhaps in this biosphere alone in all its forms: liquid , solid and gas. Like air and with it, water goes around, through the time-space of earthed runnels, clouded vapors, and glacial ice. The living world is its cycling pump, the energy transforms that propel it and its metamorphosis. Cells practice their fecund chemistry in its warmth, the growth streamed to tissues for kinetic pulse. Thermal vapors wave atmospheric currents and thermohaline winds form great rivers in the seas. There are none, none among all of our relatives, most beloved, who are not flung willing or un into this turbulent dance, filtering and pumping to their own metabolic swing, drinking their surfeit from the common stream.

Only the living world cares for water, requires it and is thereby required. We can choose to sacrifice our care for any purpose and at any alter we like, and have done so. For many ventured and vaunted reasons, we believe our care for water to be subordinate to some greater purpose of the moment, usually our thirst for power, its mines, hydropower dams, nuclear reactors. But in the end, it's always the same: We believe this because we think it profits us to do so. If we acknowledged our relatives, our common equity, we'd know different.

We're water looking at itself and seeing only the advertisement we've created. We build machines to filter the effluent from machines, from our homes. We have the handle, the switch, the gate, turning a watery exchange on and off...on and off.

We never left the water, never left the sea. All of our cells still nest here in its tributaries.

≈

Fire

HEAT IS THE CATALYST, THE AXIS ON WHICH THE living world cycles through darkness and light, dissipation and renewal. Is it gravity or heat and light that draw us, earth, to the source? A living world must always in some semblance choose life.

No human attribution this, but a common sentiment, and for this living earth life is born in the arms of the sun's orbit. Free, nearly limitless energy. What living world could turn it down? None, as it turns out. However we might equate it, through any measure, scope or lens we might invent, no life grows from entropic equilibrium; only in its collapse, its dissipation and renewal through fire's gate, the horizon that calls us. The living world is formed on this wheel, its chemistry and physiology of cells, planets, solar systems and galaxies expressing the relation, our respective eyes lit, our bodies shadowed in the holographic heat.

We are fruitfully multiplying in a gradient, an attenuated interval in the pattern of earthly temperature. These biospheric shallows, the warm, salted and oxygenated bath in which we pad and paddle about, is a rare gift, a thermal trough, a fertile valley in a brief planetary summer. The metabolic time in which the great planet moves encompasses our moment in perhaps a breath. Like light, our language bends with the continuum, and is out of sight beyond the horizon. Yet the living world speaks with us as for all our relatives, if we listen.

We build cold models, quarried on patriarchal ground, their logic strung to extrapolate events beyond our scope and animate their golems in created worlds. This is of limited use to the living world, constantly dissipating and emerging in newly forming thermodynamic relationships. It's our own use that has concerned us. Finding a sun's free energy too common, and insufficient to industrious civilizing, we've pillaged the living world to stoke enlisted fire, charging each other for the privilege of its propertied radiance.

Ignoring our own thermal pulse, that of the living world, we look about for what else we might usefully burn. Pyromaniacs on a planet of carbon life forms, we've generalized (a bit of linguistic neutering) and commoditized (a bit of economic neutering) most of our relatives into "biomass," the new and most promising fuel for our furnaces.

Fire has left its heat in us, most beloved, as in all others of the living world. We cradle our children, each other, all of our loves, in this warmth. We also fuel and flare its other aspect, the swung gate, its death's-head, in this guise consuming ourselves and all in its path. We choose our orbit.

Anima

WHAT MOVES THE LIVING WORLD, EMERGING IN
and among us, self-organizing and selflessly dis-
organizing? We round and rise on this wheel, but
are discomfited and divide to conquer, partition-
ing to scale, until we have nanofied our universe
before us and are standing empty-handed, a cos-
mological constant, in the vacuum of our own
making. Or conversely, we scope the multiverse,
time-shifted to hindsight, to gauge the future
from a present known only as our own, the vast
remainder of the living world background to our
inscribed histories, the sporting events known as
civilizations. Yet we move, most beloved, waves

of cells, bodies, herds and forests, cities, every expressed collective bloomed in ancient tides, and on the backswing, shoaled in their ebb to salt the sediments for the return, the collapsed release, the long contraction drawn through stone. We move, with or without thought, human or inhuman, move earth, air, water and fire into the shapes that spin this day against its amassed thermodynamic core, all there is of us, the living world moving.

For every code we proscribe, every mapping or sequence, every measure of logic, there is a universe swarming out of our nets. We've attempted to capture its movement in models philosophical, mechanical, algorithmic, genomic and molecular, celebrating our successes upon acculturated pedestals arranged for the purpose, little noticing the entire living world loping insouciant down the road, stopping only to urinate on our dahlias.

What is our explanation that we must have one at all cost? Have we gone arrhythmic and are attempting to resync? Perhaps an electro-chemical repulsion, Mesmer's opposite, pulsing us from shadowed depth into reflection? Whatever the reason for question, the asking, the need to ask is a movement in expansion, one answered in the contracted return. This is anima, the living world, how we know and are known. All that is living, at any scale, has this expression of ebb and flow, expansion and contraction, illumined and shadowed, amplified and reduced, the swinging gate.

Given a pattern our wont is to purpose it to our benefit, a singular enterprise, enlarging our stamped collection to tool logic, yet the living world denies us the satisfaction. True, there are transitory successes accomplished in a duration of the pendulum's arc, enough for short-timers seeking to profit (by definition) beyond their full measure, and thereby removing from others in the living world theirs. Such celebrated and destructive bursts do occur. But the pattern of ebb and flow is aperiodic, having no dependable duration wholly because it is, after all, a living world, a storied multidimensional web of relationships at any moment emerging newly pulsing life within, among and around itself.

We turn away, after the moment of recognition, when our arc is expended, our quested oscillation reverting its phase, time-space and heat-shifted, and the return begins, a gratefully eased release like coming home.

Don't Mention the Turtle

IF ONCE THE EARTH DID RIDE ON THE BACK OF A great turtle, we have quite lovely photos proving that without a doubt this is not now the case. Although we cannot prove the turtle was never there, we assume, having found no evidence of planet- bearing turtles elsewhere, that this is so. Also, it is ludicrous. So, we'll not speak of it again. After this. Then we'll certainly entertain the subject no further.

There is a famous story that has been often told and just as often misrepresented. At the end of a William James lecture, in which he had described the empirical view of the solar system, a small, wrinkled and exceedingly insignificant old lady in black stood up and said, "What you have told us is a fine story, but you seem to think it is real. You have forgotten that in the oldest story, the earth is supported on the back of a giant turtle." Dr. James smiled and asked what then was supporting the turtle. "Why, it's turtles all the way down, my boy," she replied.

We have found that although no giant turtle is to be seen supporting the earth, neither is anything else to be seen doing so, which has led us to assume it is nothing all the way down. Except for gravity, which may or may not be something. Though we have no photos of gravity either, it is the word we have decided to use (instead of "turtle", for example) to refer to that thing which cannot be seen, nor proved to exist except by inference, by its effect, yet is attractive enough to be chosen to support everything in the universe, including, apparently, the time-space continuum, which the universe never goes anywhere without.

The "turtles all the way down" story is generally misunderstood to be an excellent example of infinite regression, one of the horns of the

Münchhausen Trilemma. This misapprehension is due to the story being told almost solely by and for empiricists, a much straightened society often captivated by linear interpretations. Even so, the difficulty, well one of the rather many difficulties, in the empirical perspective is in assuming that there is a sequence of turtles, rather than a continuum. Although, again, it is just a whim, a foolish gesture, we might assume that if space or time can be a continuum, so too might other representations, such as life, periodically celebrated as a great turtle. Ridiculous, of course, but logically infallible, unless you are a fallibilist, in which case, it is no more ridiculous than anything else.

The point the old lady was making, and which sailed brazenly past the esteemed philosopher, most beloved, was that the only thing supporting the earth is a larger expression of the living world itself, rather well cast as a great turtle. Take that away, and gravitational fields may still waltz in spacetime, but in any case, less empirically so without its appreciative audience.

❧

Stone and Memory

WHAT MEMORIES THE LIVING WORLD HAS, SHARP-flaked obsidian, stream-smoothed limestone, mountains of earth-hammered granite, seas of memory-salted bodies, of skies lifted in clouds of water, salmon returning home, migrations of memories; our own that we would hold apart, but are mindful of only through those others of the living world. What memories we take, mined and hewed from the body that holds them, cherished, clenched into itself, to its burning heart. Cherished as our own children. How could they not be? Drawn to stone, through millennial sediments, immense pressures, cores of heat to the enthalpic embrace that with its sun forms and feeds us all.

As no other species, we alter to our purpose: cleft mountains, shift rivers, bore and tunnel to mine the lithosphere, shaping our futures from ancient memories. Above all we seek the those most potent, their dense energies, the hydrocarbons to slake power's thirst. Our rigs raising the oil, we've turned our attentions again to the carbonized rock within our reach, beheading mountains or shattering slopes in coastal watersheds; and to the gases encased in stone, their shells burst, fracked and fissured by injected torrents.

What becomes of a stone's memories, the trajectories of moments that has gathered to it? What's lost in what we take, and in the remorseless taking of everything between us and our claimed purpose. Everything separating us from our desire becomes debris, fragments of meaning, riven from its own pathways, its relatives, surfaced before its moment, exposed to elements and atmosphere upon a wholly different wheel of the living world, before its memoried intent can be accomplished. We've no conception of what is lost.

Perhaps our memories too lie in that debris, all we find useless. What do we know of the plants, our great-great-grandmother's medicines, their way of growing and healing, their needful web of relatives? What of tracking our way by starlight, by the living air, the scents of water, tree and soil, by the moving and morphing anima? What do we know of when to choose and when to change? What do we know of what the stones remember?

These larger memories do not belong to us. We share in them, most beloved, in life and in death, our part necessary too beyond our scope. All our relatives, all ancestors, find their way through earth and stone, and we do not honor them. Power consumes us before our time, exposing us to its fumes, our relatives falling, lost to our memories, all of us hastened to stone.

Islands

WHAT'S UNDER US ARE CARBONIFEROUS ROOTS.
Up above, it's all air and water, sunlight between.
A mountain is an island made so by water. A
mountain or an island may change places, though
usually beyond the compass of our metabolic
time. We fit the living world into language based
on perceived categories. Unlike fish, we can't exchange the water in which an island grows for
that of a mountain's air. Our lives grow under
air, rather than water. We have that in common
with a mountain, and so name it differently when
it bathes. Leap off an island and we're floated
on the liquid thermals to continental shelves,
one of nature's organizing principles. A different

organizing principle applies when we leap off mountains. So, we've found it useful to distinguish among our relatives in the living world categorically. If, to our mind, organisms or objects have enough in common, we can treat them as the same thing. 'Course there's nothing inherently human about this. Apparently, all other creatures on earth, perhaps all other organisms, have studied this methodology as well and have come to the same conclusion.

During the Enlightenment, the West noticed that we could apply this methodology to extraordinary effect simply by persisting until we could find no more shared characteristics. The traditionalists were perplexed by this overwhelming reliance on reduction and redundancy. It all seemed rather OC at the time, but they figured it was just a phase the species was going through. We learned in this way to take things apart and put them back together, to build entirely new things from categorical bits, to manipulate as one a collection of many. We found that everything could be an island, a thing known solely in terms of the category in which we placed it. We learned, believed we learned rather, that the categories we

discovered thereby gave us categorical dominion, and we extended what had after all been a
fairly rudimentary created world into one vastly
complex. Presently, we decided there's something
so fundamental that it's universal and unifying.
Back to the beginning.

There are troublesome effects with this empirically successful approach. Not the least of
them being that collecting things around their
shared characteristics misses the individual relationships, which as we are rediscovering, are
critical. An ecosystem, for example, is so highly specified in its relationships that it functions
very nearly as a host organism, a characterization
widely applied to our planet as well. That we are
capable of identifying only a small range of these
relationships in any ecosystem is a tribute to our
reductive abstractions. After all, a category is an
abstraction, a number of things in general and
none in particular.

We've wondrously reduced the living world,
most beloved, redacting it into periodic bits fundamental to our purposes, proving common de-
nominators to our common selves. Yet it's in the
uncommon, the fecund diversity, that we uncat-

egorically emerge, each of us uniquely borne in our web of relations. And it's our widely shared roots, in earth, sunlight, air and water that make it possible for us to be so, both island and mountain.

Maps

THE UNIVERSE CAME TO US UNMEASURED, WITH-
out map or compass, calendar or clock. Figuring
out where you are in time-space is a matter of
contrast, of describing relationships. Where you
are is everywhere you are not. Not very useful
from this singular perspective, though. To be
more discrete, you'd need something that could
express the common time-space that's in between
you and every other thing, without reference to
any of the near-infinite distinctions, the quali-
ties that make each relationship unique. 'Course
there's nothing like that blooming in the whole
living world. Perhaps a representation, something created would be best, something abstract

that wouldn't become bogged down in the fecund morass of life.

A way to quantify the time-space that happens between you and any arbitrary relationship, say that tree outside your window, would be most useful. This particular time-space may be filled with all kinds of intriguing events. The life stories of incalculable numbers of beings may be occurring and recurring simultaneously in that interregnum of your metabolic here and there. Still, we'd never get anywhere with our measure of success if we allowed ourselves to be distracted by those less directed to our interests. Quantification is the arbiter, linguistically sterile and applicable to all relationships without distinction, variance or favor, except ours, of course, our favor: one to nothing.

There were unquantifiable difficulties for awhile as we worked this. For one thing, almost nobody believed in the existence of nothing: zero was a ridiculous concept to folks, both in terms of space and time. Since in the West at least, the I-Three was everywhere and always, there couldn't be a place or time where there was nothing. And the existence of zero was unfortunately impossible to prove in either case, except using the same abstract framework in which it was posited, which seemed a bit circular even to medievalists. Eventually, it was revealed that this very circularity was manifest in planetary orbits, which connected the Hand to the dots and assuaged the nonheretics.

There were other issues for the ponderous and recalcitrant to hurtle, like what unit of measurement we might stamp upon measureless space (the English inspiration was the king's foot), the auspicious moment upon which to found a calendar and how to figure out when that was without one, and what chronological events might be recognizable standard bearers in the river of ceaseless time (the clerics were the only ones with a routine which they felt all should emulate). But all in all, measuring proceeded apace and we began to find ourselves in locations that would fit on postcards.

Finding rather too diverting his reliance on inebriated merchant sailors for geographical details, Mercator, exuding an aroma of Portuguese invention, finessed a metaphorical fishing net to wrap around the entire earth, marrying lat and longitudinal abstractions to a model of coherence that would fish and cut bait. Perhaps the first model that scaled sufficiently, as well.

Maps have a spatial flavor to us, but this reflects only the civilization's imperial obsession with the more physical of the time-space aspects, as well as its perspective on utility. How does a map of time offer time itself to our manipulative improvements? This particular abstraction has taken awhile to emerge, but is feeding back as we speak and transforming the created world much as spatial maps did. Perhaps its clearest visage is in the deployment of the genetic engineering imperial fleets to colonize evolutionary processes.

Where you are depends on what you believe. To know where you are in common and verifiable terms, you have to accept some authority that defines your relationship to all other things in time-space. For example, we have the time of our lives by plotting our metabolic moment against that of a decaying atom. Its accuracy is a function of the relationship's vast time-space difference. Nothing authoritative here, yet it points in that direction so satisfactorily that we make the seemingly perennial mistake of figuring the pointy bit is the authority itself. Although, theoretically, this acceptance of authority can be utilitarian, a working hypothesis, in practice it generally acquires the more enduring character of belief. We've a functional, if not sacral belief that there is an absolute somewhere and time upon which measures of time-space can be hung.

Our current spatial version of the pointing finger is GPS, a multidimensional, uniscaling grid on which you (or anyone else) can exact your represented self from any space. We always know precisely where we are, or someone does or can. Comforting, in a way. No more worries then about where we might be and all that. We've flipped the auto-pilot and are sipping tea while the tempo and terrain whizzing by are time and space shifted to local measure.

So, there you have it. It took a few centuries, but we've managed to map ourselves into some semblance of order. There are a few strays and wandering nitwits, but most are safely aboard. No more tedious trips to oracles or playing a cosmic version of Where's Waldo. 'Course it is a figment, but no less so than any other, and it's one most all agree on, which makes it rather appealing, doesn't it?

There is another way of locating ourselves. Particularly useful when something's amiss and the edifices delineating our claims are showing fractures. Doesn't come with Good Civilization's seal of approval, of course, but it does work, at least if history is any measure. Use the continuum. It's still there under our overlay of maps and measurements, as time and spacely omnific as ever. Doesn't have any of the strictures or comforts of our imagined home, of course, and locating yourself in a continuum is less distinguished. It took the ancients a while to get the hang of it. They had to attend to all the relationships, the ones between here and there, between us and that tree outside our window. They had to lose their metabolic point of view, their human-centric measure of things. They learned "inhuman" was not a pejorative, and in fact, as for "human," was wholly unquantifiable and immeasurable in value. They found that where they were was also where everything else was. They found all their relatives. They found humility.

Their language had to accommodate itself to the continuum as well. Language is a map too, though a living one, the meta-map used to represent time and space, the relationships that arose. It had to adapt to the immense feedback. Relationships are reciprocal, and that between language and a measureless living world had to find its equilibrium. New areas, ranges of reference emerged. You can find bits of all this in the old stories and what we refer to as ancient art, in traditions that made common in space and time the interests and actions of the people with that of all the relatives.

You can find this again, most beloved, the place where we may yet be.

❧

The Territory

WHAT NO MAP CAN CONVEY IS USELESS, IS USE-lessness. The path of a bird to a geologist, the extent of a coal seam to an ornithologist. What we do not intend, where our intent has no scope is trackless, beyond our Cartesian graphs and grams, beyond any measure, any rule, beyond any representation, even thought, we might make of it. What is so useless that we cannot conceive of it? There is no greater question than this, because herein lies the territory, the timeplace that is our bearing in the living world.

The efficacy of a map, a representation, de-rives from its lack of unintended, useless information, and from its incompleteness. Every increase in its approximation, in the model's proximate relation and resemblance to its subject, creates entropy, the representation shedding its value, its information, as it approaches the presentation itself: the living world.

Yet we are so taken by our maps and models that we often mistake them for their subject, the thing itself, or perhaps we prefer it so, finding intended value more capably in the manageably incomplete, the measurably useful.

And what is the path of a passing swan to a geologist coring for coal? The relationship may escape our utility, but there it is, called into being, a story that may one day tell itself.

It's useless to attempt to contain an unbounded reciprocating process, the lesson of the sun, its messages life-bearing information slipping through our hands, filling our shadow, transforming all and thereby transformed. It's useless to expect to rule where everything recapitulates something else, the genomes of ancestors carried to offspring, the ancestry developing in accordance to new and emerging relations; the cultural body of language prescribing our habitation, its words spoken or written into movements reshaping the language itself.

What is lost to representation doesn't mean it isn't expressed. There is nothing more expressive than the useless. This is its power, most beloved, the immeasurable moment that impoverishes us with its wealth, dislodges our words, takes away our breath. It's also useless to name it, though we do, reducing to our scales measure this treasure, this death-defying beauty wielding life naked-edged, this territory.

Passage

To a passenger, the landscape through which one moves is a continuum. Objects are distinguishable until velocities and neural synapses pack up their picnic baskets and move on. That which appeared as landscape is irrevocably altered by the passage, though the passenger's attentions have grown indifferent, a calloused paramour. Passengers, after all, can only transit, without engaging the nature of their attentions. 'Course, we may disembark, lovely old nautical accompaniment, immediately losing passenger status and becoming part of the landscape, another of its objects. "Oh, look dear, there's a native." And there are the passengers, passing, a parallel continuum blurring through our re-sounding landscape.

Well, not our landscape, but one we share with the other *objets d'arte*. Our claim, one of belonging, rather than ownership. Our certification has been stamped and authorized by the authorizers. There's the gate. We step off the platform.

There's a vaguely soft insistence rubbing against us like sleep and memory, a breeze with antennae. When you look around to see, there's just the sky breathing across the landscape, a landscape to which we return, wondering. There it is again. Let's take a walk.

We've forgotten we belong here, arriving this day only through artifice. Maybe that's why we feel awkward and out of place. The baggage we're carrying, so efficient for passengers on the bus of civilization, seems ridiculous, weighted with fine irrelevance. Let's leave it.

Look, there's where you fell off the swing. Here's where we lay in the grass and drew clouds into cartoons. There's the old spring, its water sweet and cold. The carved stones that grew fragrant in the rain. The birds that sang us awake. The lakes that held us. The rivers that carried us.

The ancestors everywhere gone to earth, water, air and fire.

We're remembered here though, our leavings a desolate swathe through this embodied community, one now being reclaimed by arching trees, celebrants, their roots lifting and cracking lichen-etched pavement, dandelions and mosses thriving in the fissures.

Grown foreign, we can hear the clear laughter at our misguided stumbling, its music shaking the leaves as we move below the canopy. Yet it is, without mistake, a welcome.

It has always called, that soft insistence, needing us too. The memory of its voice deep in ours, our hands, our passage. This place that meets and joins us.

Roads

WHAT IS IT THAT WANTS A ROAD? FEET CHOOSE other paths, oddly mapped habituations that like streams gravitate across terrain with the certainty of drunken wanderers. For most of those now living, the world came to us on roads. It wasn't always so. For millennia, roads were few, short and narrow. To the horizon, from nearly any mountain or ridge, no roads carried us, brought us home, took us away, as far as you could see. The world we carried with us was larger because it didn't have as far to go.

What is there between the places that mark our knowledge, that we know only as distance? A direction calling itself a road, joining by its relation wherever it impinges. But a road is purposeful beyond its casual relations. It's a weighty proposition, a hammered pact we've made with our destinations. And where the road touches us, where we enter the medium, we are connected as surely as if it were an appendage. When there is no off switch, when every place, every home, is routed to every other place, what is there that is not the medium? We live on roads, physical and virtual.

As Rome told us, an empire lives by its roads. No roads, no empire. Rome made roads to last forever. The current empire, finding planned obsolescence generates greater production, makes roads to a different standard. Among the many bequests of the second World War was an appreciation for rapid transport and redundant supply lines. Military strategists with time and a government on their hands constructed a highway system. Dependably homogeneous and built for speed, maps and towns lost each other, the spoken roads no longer familiar. Bankers and oil companies harnessed urban planners to map geometries of roads and houses into cheapened rural environs, taking out full page spreads for the

American Dream. The sweet and slow idiosyncratic lives lost their snap in the face of such unbridled anonymity. Bide-A-Wee motel and Morris Super Rose gas station followed the southern gothic into an engineered decline.

The new roads imparted measured distance to ancient energy. Fossils may have fueled a million years, but how far can they go in an hour? A civilization that lives on the road insists on immediacy or it will take its gratification elsewhere. Another road, another town, another site, all having an oddly familiar look.

When roads are all interconnected, most beloved, they are one endless road, having no distinction between everywhere and nowhere. We're mainlining more, better, faster, larger roads. Through them we look for the connections that will deliver us to the immediacy we once knew, when the world did not come with roads, but opened clear as a bell all around us.

Property

PROPERTY USED TO BE A MADE THING, POSSESSED
for its value or utility, and with an equivalent lifespan. You knew where it came from, could hold it
or trade it, watching it depart with a new owner.
At an axial point in the history of a hard- working
civilization, property leaped into the metaphoric
arms of an abstract construct, a mentalist's trick
of embodiment, acquiring in us a private estate,
one we fondly call our own, though the question
of ownership has always been ambiguous.

Property was quite expressive, and finding in
us a medium of omnivorous proportions, it became more expansive, acquiring an exhilarating
breadth and capacity. Most assuredly, it found its

desire in land, a marriage so felicitous that these two acquired a common definition. This property-land collusion was a private conversation, and came as a shock to those of us who weren't included.

When Europeans wandered into the new-to-them worlds, they brought property-land along for the ride, and carefully explained to soon to be uninhabitants just what it was and how you use it. Seemed like those of us who were natives were a bit thick on that point, figuring maybe it was a game of some sort, like hide the pea, since obviously you couldn't buy land. Who would you pay? Maybe if we played along for awhile, we could get back to doing what most sane adults normally do in their free time.

It took awhile for the millions of us living there to fully appreciate the property-land concept. Turned out, this was one of those game-changers. To play, people and their place, their field of play, had to be differentiated, separable units... odd, that. What could you be other than this life among all your relatives? If you didn't play, you had to leave the field, and the game was always played on your home field. After the dust had cleared, those of us still standing were escorted off, wondering what just happened.

Although fond of land, property can be, and is, nearly anything. Having mapped a world of land and water to property's dominions, we carefree property-labeling OCs have rubberstamped our way across the living world, property biggering itself, Seussian-wise, until everything has or soon will be commoditized: earth, air, water, blood, genomes, molecules. If you can be useful in any potentially conceivable way, property wants you, redundantly so, apparently. Some property is derived from itself, a tail-engorging bit of work that's not yet completed its disappearing act.

'Course for it to be your officially certified property, you have to actually own it. Property is an exercise in privacy, or perhaps it's vice versa. Nonetheless they're hip-joined sack-racers. If it's private, it's a declaration of property, allotted in some personal or civil consensus. 'Course there's public property, the republic's all for one/one for all franchise. Yet property still, and bounded to a publican's measure. If it's not property, it can't be owned, and all that can be owned is property. The origin of this utilitarian principle is difficult to trace, yet the adage to follow the money seems fruitful.

Ascertaining whether you actually own a property is generally simpler than our institutions would have you think. You don't. Most of us own very little, instead are ourselves owned, our future value pledged in exchange for the civil self in which lies our current commodity. Much of what we consider our property...house, land, car, and more...is only an advertisement for future ownership. Seems real enough, this appearance of property, but lacks the presence, the resonance of affirmation to bring it on home...to the home that we had, that wasn't property at all. Maybe that's why so few of us have one any more.

Where we are, most beloved, there is only the living, the dead moving through their long honored transformation. Property, as we've known it, is a construct, a word and story we've used to privatize the living, acquiring all our relatives and our very selves. Its strength or its frailty lies only in our gift, the place of recognition.

❧

Debts

ALL THAT WE HAVE IS DEBT, RECEIVED OR AC-
quired to sustain us, as true in the civilly created
world as it is in the living world. To live is to be
indebted in some medium of exchange, whether it
be money, goods, services, or resources. All such
exchanges derive from the living world, our very
breath received from relatives in the biosphere,
though either through ignorance or hubris we
rarely acknowledge this source, nature's central
bank, preferring to recognize these as gifts or in-
herited rights, without obligation or recourse.

The living world of course doesn't work that
way. Accounts are kept and balanced continu-
ously. We ignore opportunities of repayment, and

forgetful that we are ourselves an expression of the living world, neglect to notice our debts are being collected in and around us. The health of our communities then becomes precarious, a litany of environmental damage and degradation amplified through feedback loops and moving through biogeochemical cycles, our debts increasing exponentially. Our own health, our living solvency, is integrated with that of all our relatives, and our ecological community bereft of our needed payments, is thereby reduced and afflicted.

Everything we have put to our use, all that we have produced, our own populous selves, must be accounted for and appropriate recompense made to the living world. This fundamental knowledge, missing in a civilization, is what folks once gave their children in stories and in a way of life. To do otherwise is to lose the balance upon which the lives of ourselves and our communities depend. Every culture has old stories of what comes to restore balance, none of them pleasant.

Drawn on nonhuman and human resources, debt is what a sovereign sells, what banks produce, what citizens acquire. Its promissory note is the currency of the realm. It's repackaged and re-sold in euphemistic financial instruments, a virtu-al reincarnation. Without it there'd be no invest-ment, no hats to pull profit out of, and we would all have considerably less, those few with the most, most considerably so. Debt is our future, the measure of faith in human commerce and progress, its size in the global economy dwarf-ing the combined GDPs of all countries many times over. To imagine a world without it is to be ridiculed, to seriously propose such, sacrilege. It would mean the end of the known civilization, presumably.

It's difficult to see around or past such a monolith, the view encompassed and colored by its influence. Only recently is ecological econom-ics receiving any consideration, is a full account-ing of human enterprise in the living world being mentioned, new models proposed to interpret our commerce within the entire community, to translate the relationships of ecology into the val-uations of economics. In this we are attempting a transition, yet the difficulty is that all payments in the living world are in kind, at a valuation determined by the ecological community, and amortized over a metabolic range equal to that of the debt. Pretending for a moment an equal valuation for all trees in a community, the use of a twenty-five year old tree is one for which we could feasibly make compensation, while the use of a fossil fuel millions of years old is one for which we cannot, not in any community.

The questions, the hinges on which civilizations, sovereigns, corporations, communities and we artfully swing, are whether to acknowledge this debt, and if so, how it can be satisfied. The answers, most beloved, depend on the balance we seek.

Profit

WHAT IS LEFT AT THE END OF THE DAY, ANY MEA-
sure of time in which we find our sustenance?
What is left to hold our promise into all that is
beyond us? Is it enough what we hold dear at
that dimming, enough to ease our rest, our ebb
that will return us here to the gift that is this
timeplace? We've thought this to be our question,
but it's not. It's the living world that asks, asks
in its becoming, in us, and what answer we may
have is carried stream to river to sea, among all
of our relatives, all members of our community.
What profits us bears promise into uncertainty,
and must do so for the whole community as well,
or all are thereby impoverished.

Enough...beyond a moment, we can never know with certainty what this is, this relationship between what we need and what we have. It's what sustains our ongoing participation, the transforming metabolic energies which carry our fundamental relationships in our community. In traditional cultures, local communities that evolve in the absence of a civilization, profit is the result of opportunism, yet always within this larger sustaining participation. To do otherwise would be understood to harm the community, the super-organism on which all members depend. The very presence of The People, the only distinction a human traditional culture ever need make of itself, is an acknowledgement of this understanding, their stories its telling.

From our current perspective, wealth amassed and securely held would appear to give favorable odds to always having enough, hence the civilization, and our embodiment of its thought. 'Course to get these odds requires a decrease in our contributions to the sustenance of the community and an increase in our predation. How this is accomplished may vary across civilizations, but because it eventually impoverishes any community in which it is applied, this works to best advantage at a remove from the communities that provide such profit. A civilization manufactures a cultural community, a created world to sever the old relationships, to replace the old stories honoring all the relatives with stories of the civilizing culture, and sustains itself by progressively draining the ecological wealth of the communities on its peripheries. The current civilization is pinioned to its corporations, entities residing only in their legal fiction, visiting their nowhere upon every community entered. Seeking profit, we are assured, is a civilized entitlement, and one that eventually benefits all.

What is this profit that in our time finds as its most telling feature the sixth extinction of all species on earth? What or whom among all our rapidly disappearing relatives is such profit to benefit? What does profit support if not the most fundamental of our relationships in the living world?

Although most economists would protest, every profitable measure is an isolate derived from some investment of labor or capital, describing the remains of such investment at some given time, its expression and manifest traded in the markets and exchanges, in a sovereign's bond and currency. Only profit's aggregate increase is of value, because who would seek loss? Yet our loss is so great. Scoped to any of the entire communities in which profit is sought, communities at such remove that we can speak of them only by modifying common usage: the ecological community of our time and place, all that gives us our home. This community, though we may not remember it in its fullness, as it thrived once with us, if we see it clearly now as it is, we will find it has little measure in our accounting. Our profit has produced generations of deficit here, in this place, most beloved, in the only home this earth can offer us. What profits us?

Poverty

CLEAR AS AIR OUR LIFE COMES TO US, YET WHEN we are denied a sufficiency and cannot thrive, we then know as we must the face of our poverty.

In a civilization where wealth is so clearly and relentlessly advertised as money and power, as what these can acquire for us, poverty is its lack. Whether or not we can avoid such poverty, most of us make efforts to avoid its appearance, for the appearance of a thing is to us evidence enough. We see only difference, and when the poster child is wealth, all that varies from this image bespeaks degrees of separation, appearance its word already spoken. This poverty, this civilized poverty, is one we have created and sustain to measure our creation, our progress. We rise beyond this, we think to rise beyond this, through education, persistent work, genius, art, cunning, or force; through any means available, or perhaps any necessary, as our heroes and anti-heroes evince. This is a powerful poverty that we visit upon ourselves. Let's walk away for a moment, leaving it suspended on our belief. It'll be there when we return.

Unaccompanied by our civil and commercial poverty, the physical necessities are obvious: clean air and water, honest food, shelter and clothing. The availability of clean air and water is certainly questionable, as is food earth-given and free of industrial solutions. We adapt to such conditions, and our efforts strain first the health of the weakened, yet the depth, the intensity of our adaptations always appear most noticeably in our children. An inability to thrive metabolically and through generations is a poverty without peer, all other considerations of wealth meaningless. Our metabolic health, our survival, depends solely on those of our relatives who synthesize sunlight to produce the air and carbon we transform. Their loss is ours, our poverty, and in this the sixth extinction, their loss is great.

Our logic, our science has an inherent bicameral inclination, an either/or persuasion reflected in the prongs of the nature versus nurture contention that has plagued us. Nature is nurture, and what it nurtures is itself, us inseparable from our community; nurtures what is our shared wealth, that we may thrive, that we are not impoverished. We express this, are expressions of this living world, nurturing our children and each other to such intent. Beyond lack of physical sustenance, what then does the living world tell us of our poverty?

What of communion, community, commons? We are poor in what we share in sense, in kind, in understanding, in our telling, the stories that shape us together. We have become disparate, monoculturing, insatiate and lost to the great diversity of our common wealth.

And of our timeplace? We have measured this continuum into units of trade, labor and capital, into allotments of private property, dominions of power and belief. We exist and move in these, our cells, our models, our containments that describe the exchanges creating wealth and poverty.

What of beauty? All of our senses give us information, a description of energy, and seek to gratify us thereby; a gesture of desire, a longing for living beauty.

Such beauty cannot be held or contained, yet in our hubris we think to do so, and while wreaking destruction of its living embodiment with one hand, with the other we'd create cultural replicas, and expend fortunes to fill our cities and towns, our homes in the attempt to thwart this impoverishment.

Of peace? We presume to bring, to offer, to instill peace, thinking it a thing separate from its place, a product of some human process or institution. We wish for peace while removing from our places the only relationships, the only communities in which it can occur. Peace doesn't belong to us, and grows only in community, in our practice in an honored place, and grows now poorly.

And wisdom? There is much we can acquire, have again proved this civilizing characteristic, but we can't acquire what can't be grasped, generally dusting such phantoms into children's stories. Wisdom, like beauty and peace, can't be obtained, but is an attentive participation in our place, listening to all our relatives; a practice we hold in small regard, a great poverty.

No poverty is complete in its privation, but is an insufficiency, a failing to thrive. There are many faces of our poverty, and we must know them, most beloved, understand their influence, so guiding us to the wealth that is the birthright of all in the living world.

❧

Consumers

WE CANNOT BUY OWNERSHIP, ONLY PROPERTY. Ownership is a private matter in a public place. Legality is an *ex post facto* argument, and one compromised by its consistent lack of democratic civility. Possession, as they say, is nine-tenths of it. Let's out this antiquated notion plainly. At our juncture in the Western imperium, none among us owns anything we buy, nor ever will. We have acquired a right to consumption only, perhaps an exclusive right, reserved for our estimable use by an indifferent consensus, the rights and domain captured in writing that we may invoke the once divine, the envisioned word...so it is written. In the commons, a word written or spoken has equal resonance. This homespun agreement has since been discarded for a privileged semantics, its furtive gestures traced and tracked by solicitous guardians.

Once a common effort, a thing made by hand is now a quaint articulation, residing in reservations artful or iconic. It contravenes the social contract: a consumer does not produce. We live in the hive of the empire, sharecroppers among the monoliths, awaking and clocking in to the thrumming metabolism of commutable consumer farms. The product of our consumption is our expended energy, the fuel of the civilization, at one time seventy percent of GDP in the States. Without it, the imperial march stumbles and wobbles. Successive leaders exhort us to consume more and save the empire, a consumer-charged light brigade.

We would have exhausted our consumption long ago, had our ability to abstract and objectify not risen to the occasion. Of every element of the living world we have made a commodity shaped to one of the many forms of our consumption. We've conceived algorithms, methodologies, patents, copyrights, financial instruments, and corporations to capture the iterations our technology enables, and so consume the same thing endlessly. Anything that we cannot in some manner consume is worthless to us and thereby endangered.

We are compelled to this consumption by centuries of imperial progress, in its global ubiquity the most successful civilization ever recorded. We're an occupying force, released upon the world by an impulse we yet embody. Little need for our leaders to urge us to greater feats of consumption. This herd moves, a plague of Black Fridays, across every terrain imaginable, carrying our manifest to the unwritten, evoking the benefits of eternal consumption to countenance our purges. We are the armies of an insatiate civilization, recognizing nothing of the commons, consuming our very lives and that of our children.

We were more than this, most beloved...we can be more than this.

Food

As all things seek their level, life aspires to food. The earth can be, and indeed was, ebullient with food, procreating like a natural, seasonally, of course, but locally as well, in this way contributing the diverse bodies, the many hands that each in their distinction, together through their differences, through dearth and surfeit, help flux the living world, the sustaining pulse.

Civilizations find this variability insufficient to power's appetite, and devote their energies to discovering and correcting earth's inadequacies. This occurs sporadically however, because despite their contentions of progress, civilizations are entropic backsliders like everyone else.

Western civilization is particularly successful in its food divertissement. This genome rode cattle and wheat out of the Fertile Crescent and has been circumnavigating the globe, selling beef on a bun ever since. The diet and its supportive, largely uncelebrated bacterial symbionts produced an empiric energy that discovered everything anew, putting it all into ever so much better containers like a happy gaggle of home-canners.

An ethos that builds officious monoliths to the small god of productivity works wonders when applied to that old chestnut, food. Turns out, food wasn't producing nearly as efficiently as it should. It was promiscuous, often went home early, and wandered about in disreputable company. A colorful vagabond, grant you, but one with grubby appendages and an odor. Food, it was found, was much more productive when properly sorted and organized into homogeneous tracts, monocultural expanses that scaled well, kept regular hours, and did not use foul language.

What exactly, one might well ask, was it that was being produced, and what was the measure of its success? "Food, and well, Return On Investment," respond the harbingers of results positioned over the production line, motioning us to move along. A small, wrinkled and exceedingly insignificant old woman in back shuffles forward and prods one of the suits with her cane, eying him rather too brightly, "Yes, but what is food?" The fellow looks about and finding no empirical basis for the question, assumes it was merely an unpleasant bit of noise. She turns around, and looking directly at us, incants: "Food is never one thing. Nor is it the sum of its parts. Nor is it separable from its belonging. It can be counted and measured, but is unconstrained by either. It is medicine and it is information, and this is so only because you share a life with the entire living world. It cannot be produced, only diverted, controlled for a time, until seeking its level, it changes, perhaps into food that no longer belongs with you. It is always and only living. This," she said, indicating with a wave of her hand the vast engineered geometries of food, "is no longer food, and though it appears to do, will not feed you. It is broken and adrift, having forsaken the living bonds we all share."

This is all unsubstantiated and unverified, of course, as attested by the analyzers of food substances, who are acknowledged by each other and the globalized purveyors of same to really know their stuff.

Unless, that is, you countenance a few millennia of local knowledge, the disparaged skills, the streams of many hands, this estuary of inheritance. Here, most beloved, on the tides of the living world, we are all food in our time, and find our level, our purchase, in our care.

Information

THOUGH WE SUPPOSE IT A HUMAN DISCOVERY, information precedes us, our arrival simply participating in more of the same, uniquely expressed in us as in all others mind you, this living recursion in which information finds sufficiency. Most of it eludes us as well, our limited scope, you see. We construct extensions, analogs of our senses, to sweep the spectrums for information that is possible, data unformed and fomenting in the wild. The data we gather with such tools, we feed to models that function within gated communities of algorithms, accepting only information with an invite, presentable data that conforms to our principles, our expectations of what information should be.

For millennia, we spent our considerable free time visually recording information, our narrative, on every surface, in every form, before the impetus to abstract the narrative into an incised, scripted representation took hold. We'd been reading signs, tracks, gestures, images all along. But writing narrowed the beam, was more restrictive, and gave us a profound grasp of particular information, a way to accumulate it verifiably beyond our span, for posterity, for ritual, for wealth. In writing, we found a medium so vast that all of human knowledge and history, the esteemed worthwhile bits anyway, could be stored, reviewed, blessed and accounted for. This written information is the medium and message of our science, the measure by which it is assessed.

From the newly-literate cultures, the old storyteller lineage wandered off into the mountains and literally inhospitable regions, much reduced. The literacy of script clothed and perfumed the body politic, distinguishing its members from the indiscriminate smudge of the masses. Information, wherever found, was claimed and conscripted for the greater good, the good of the greater. Traditional folks, the civilly disgraced illiterates, attempted to point out that information was rather larger than all that, but the avid information gatherers were too busy filling their pails, packs and barges to a purpose so obviously under-appreciated by those unaffiliated amateurs. These gatherers, the literally-transformed agrarians, diverted a select crew of their energies to accumulating information, and have now got certified mountains of the stuff. Knuckle bump.

Some of us get quite anxious about it all. It is our information, our responsibility, and is just asking for a little more, a little attention please. But no matter how many books, pages, tweets we read, no matter how many talking heads we watch and listen to, the hits just keep on coming. Neural pathways writhe and fizzle. Information has no twenty-four-by-seven clock, nor does it come with an off switch. We've attempted to capture something that is always on, this whirlwind we reap an aspect of the living world, infinitely recurring and subsisting only on itself. Living things require living measures, shapes and bounds fitted to dynamic change, minute or momentous adaptations. The tools of our focus, our premises, principles, representations and models, are proscribed shells, insufficient to the task, and they are ballooning, capsizing, quaking and erupting under the strain. It isn't that there's too much information, there's always just enough, just what is needed. It's the means and manner of our use. We thought it was written, that it could be so. This is the dam we must release, so information can assume its true shapes to our telling.

'Course it's unconstrained by us, passing on through, ceaselessly making the story of life itself. Information is imparted to us through our genes, cells, and senses. We transform it, most beloved, shape it for our use, ferry it across our geographies, and send it off, *bon voyage cheri*. Our food, water, air, sunlight and heat...information all. Transports and transformers themselves, we intercede to become ourselves, engender generations, and so move the narrative along, our part unwritten but learned...it can be learned.

Affinity

ONE DAY WE'LL WAKE AND FIND OURSELVES AT
the edges of the familiar, looking out across an
unknown landscape roiled by movements we
can't follow, from sources we don't recognize.
What then? There'll be those who won't notice,
who looking out, see nothing but the familiar reflected. There'll be those who see the living unknown, but turn away, holding dear the familiar.
There'll also be others, though seeing, who are
enthralled by the collective, awaiting expert or
charismatic guidance. And there'll be the ones,
stepping blind into the unknown, growing their
familiarity as they go. 'Course, membership in
any of these not so secret societies is never closed.

Many of us wander in and out among them or their variants, sometimes daily.

The familiar always moves and develops with us, no matter who or where we are. And despite, or rather, because of the best intentions of the created world to control its dynamic progenitor, there will always be times of great change, when the shape of the created world suddenly... perhaps not so sudden to those standing at the verges...when it momentously shifts, much as you might notice it is now doing. If we find ourselves in the societies of ignorance (those who ignore by nature or choice, not the pejorative cast from competing societies), we'll be lugging the familiar about, increasingly worn by the strain, yet reluctant to part with any of its semblances. Among the fortress-builders, we'll be raising defenses, reviewing strategies and acquiring tactical holy hand-grenades. In the herd societies, we'll be exchanging raised eyebrows, headshaking or other gestures of responsible inadequacy, before returning to the sustenance offered by the occupation at hand. And in the fringe societies, we'll be wandering the borders cautiously or in, poking instinctively at bits of protruding elephant, scribbling coordinates and pictograms, and waving semi-coherent semaphores as the world emerges, conceived somewhat anew.

Affinities shape both the living world and our understanding, our very ability to conceive of it. The patterns in nature form by affinity. We believe, choose and move by affinity. It is a constant across millennia, recognized by astrologists, alchemists, physicists and philosophers. It's at the distinction, where the familiar and the new or unfamiliar meet. Both attracting and impelling, it's the fundamental force of the fundamental forces, the one which humanity cannot harness.

Yet, as for everything else, affinity ebbs and flows, our relationships contracting or expanding, their constraint entropic, affinity seeking its level, its minimal equilibrium. The growth of a pattern ceases to develop then, and this becomes the timeplace where we are expended, our lives altering their expression, their form and knowledge, as new or renewed relationships develop.

Though we try, we cannot map this confluence of feedback loops. It's incredible complexity is why we cannot know what we know, most beloved, why we have only affinity to guide us, and why it has always been this way, though we are long out of practice, as we begin again to sense our way among the relatives.

The Act

IT'S ONLY IN WHAT WE DO, THE ACT, ITS IMAGING
into focus our claim to this life, that we become
the relationship we and others know as ourselves.
We act with or without knowing, on choices
thoughtful or metabolic, intended or autonomic.
We are enacted as well, across time and space by
ancestral relationships, genomes, environments,
all transmuted to our embodied moment. This
act that is of us, but so much larger, conveys us
into its moment and scope, extending far beyond
our borders.

No intended action resides only in its expression. It grows in our choosing from among the
community of possible acts, those given or creat-

ed from our relations in the living world. It opens into our motion, drawing with it our nearby relatives, and as we release it from our intent, it continues on without us until absorbed in the living expanse. Because an action has as its medium the living world, some, perhaps all, of what we do does not dissipate as we might expect, but is amplified by our relatives to surprising magnitude, a corollary to physics' butterfly effect, biology's biomagnification. Cause and effect are obscured in such continual reciprocity, as the act pulses through the reverberant web, to no horizon we can fathom.

Western rationalism, its jurisprudence, its ecclesiastical sanctions, would limit the domain of an act to its human orbit, creating a private property that is ours alone. This is a Cartesian figment, the slice and dice method to sort and apportion an objectified time-space. Nothing of what we do, none of our actions are so bounded. Such configurations are utilitarian, appearing only in the created world of these reflecting minds. It is the living world, the unbounded dynamic in which our action is expressed and resonates, that requires our full attention.

In acting we join ourselves to all our relatives. Through our intent, our choice of action, its demeanor and motion, its conveyance in time and space across the living world, through this entirety that is the act itself, we nurture and become a life grown intact and whole, or fragmented and disintegrating. The understanding that informs our intent, guides us in this potent spectrum, we had at birth, every sense capable of tuning us into range: affinity, the compass we may now perceive only vaguely.

We are not recognizable, do not exist, before we act. Death is motionless. Nor are we a prefigured constancy, an imaged personhood to nourish and defend (...by their actions you shall know them). We are life, by nature shared and negotiated, mutable and adapting, recurrently redefining ourselves by what we do.

We've thought to enlarge our action, ourselves, and thereby visit our dominion over the earth. Paradoxically, this has required making ourselves smaller, shrinking our borders to a sanctity of self, ignoring all our relatives, the movement of our actions through them, listening and speaking only to each other as approved by an objectivity scientific or divine. We need no intermediaries, most beloved. Let us be known in acts with care beyond measure, direct and well attended, both subject and object of change in a boundless life.

Objects of Faith

Etymological siblings, believed and beloved, inextricably linked, written, it's said by
some, upon the genomic face of evolution, as-
serted hypothetically as the current foundation, a
position in this civilization once occupied solely
by a monotheistic hand, one that apparently did
not include retirement in its designs, too intelli-
gent for that perhaps. Reconciling ourselves to
some telling of what, if anything, is etched upon
the fundament is the eternal pastime of those attempting, for wholly disparate and oddly con-
verging purposes, to commute present place to a
future one, preferably a comfortable passage re-
liably scheduled with good coffee and croissants.

One side of the civilized room asserts that be-lief has no objective existence. A belief that can be posited, tested, and verified by non-believers, is no longer a belief, but a working hypothesis, perhaps a pedestrian fact.

Beginning is always most difficult when what we seek is an end. Beginnings are then tiresome timeplaces where premises are so often magicked forth to vault over the occasional chasm. The ver-ifiable and objective performs a tolerable quack and waddle in the postulate of a vacuum, a suit-ably virginal locus into which hypotheses pop and figment. Human thought was birthed as subject entire, a singularity unblemished by the masses. To arrive at such a happily fertile coincident, time and space had to be cast into deified statuary. The time and space twins balanced precariously upon civil and clerical arguments, space eventually appealing to both well enough to award it the sole habitation of all objects, possession of such assigned in perpetuity to human thought (or to the civil and clerical standard bearers thereof, as deemed necessary and sufficient). Time was mea-sured and fitted for decorous pasts and futures, and enshrined in every home. All this part of the timeless strategy of civilizers, admirably applied to Freedom, Justice and other old chestnuts: win over the annoyingly intransigent by deifying them.

Although neither a timely existence nor its spatially occupied objects have arrived there yet, the future, from this pointy escarpment (the one we scaled moments ago), is written, or at least recognizably sketched, by the premises of the present. Trouble is, verifying what's written means being there to read it. Anything else is, well, a working hypothesis, which, while bearing a remarkable resemblance to a belief, posits a much more rigorous upbringing. This seems to inspire confidence in us, rather like polyphonic whistling in the dark. 'Course, you can marshal historical precedent and authoritative works to shuffle present facts into future's waiting room, and make for doing so, if not a verifiable case, a damn good one. Yet, no matter how illustrious the patina of authority, having a damn good case, is, as has been said of a recent American president, all hat and no cattle.

Meanwhile, the other side of the room says objective existence isn't the only rabbit in the hat, most assuredly isn't everything, and perhaps isn't anything at all, actually. Faith is as virginally vacuous as hypotheses any day, and functionally equivalent, working as resolutely for any person, civilization, or universe that has it. Matter of fact, belief was here first, if language is any measure, preceded etymologically only by being and desire, quietly inherent and insoluble in any hypothesis.

Belief abounds in gradations. For those more absolute occasions, it leaps into measureless faith in anyone or anything, an unbounded wonder, the leap made, as well as the territory covered, generally revisited only under duress, if at all. Beliefs of this ilk, when they occur too often, tend to result in territorial maps that have only a few large, artfully gilded blocks, surrounded by intriguing Here Be Dragons neighborhoods.

Most often, belief is a practical venture, occurring relatively rather than absolutely, content with hops rather than leaps, so you can see where you've been, where you've got to, and skip back and forth if you change your mind. To accomplish anything, acquire food, for example, we believe or hypothesize that an act is required if we are to faithfully, logically receive our entropic salvation. On the other hand, some people become so proficient at believing that they can juggle any number of flaming razor-edged beliefs with only the occasional loss of an appendage, which they generally believe they didn't need anyway.

Faith is only encumbered by the dialectic and argument dear to rational practitioners. Although providing substantial employment to clerics and evangelicals, it's ill-fitted to these traces, to convincing stratagems whose result is ever a series of literal and metaphorical cathedrals, profiting only their keepers, when a thankful nod or heartfelt hallelujah will more than suffice; indeed, all else is a redundancy. Unfortunately, because faith has insubstantial needs, it's one of those grievous irritants, an intransigence without price, something enterprising civilizers find suitable only in deities.

'Course if you look about from the commons, most beloved, we're all objects of faith and subjects of hypotheses, to others if not to ourselves; a profusion of such and more, no different in this respect than any other form of life. Only machines have a binary compulsion. The living world emerges in relationships, simultaneously subject and object, believing and believed.

Positions

EVERY ACT IS CREATION, IS INTENT FLESHED again, the intention our own or of those we enact, created into no vacuum or singularity, but into dynamic relation, negotiated into being only through those relationships that finally define the act itself. Where shall we begin? What frame of reference, set of cultural, social, psychological coordinates, what paradigm, premise, what position shall we use to describe our relations to the living world.

Western civilization has, to date, wreaked its visions of progress and development with such untroubled enthusiasm that entire species are dropping like flies, continents are terraformed to monocultural deserts, waters used to carry waste, every known biogeochemical cycle so afflicted that the biosphere itself is becoming toxic to many of its organisms. Clearly, there is no measure of accomplishment, no technological marvels, wonders of artistry or architecture, no number of filled vaults or granaries that can justify or surmount this devastation, nor equal its success, since just as clearly this civilization has achieved the dominion it ascribed to itself, felling before it all that does not reflect its image. By its actions it is known.

At this critical juncture, we are reconsidering our sustained indifference to all but human concerns, our imperial destiny. Our position has irrevocably changed, whether by choice or necessity. Where do we now stand? What is our role in the self-organizing organization that is the living world?

Recognizing where this civilization has led us in all our relations to the living world acknowledges both our complicity and our transformative understanding. As always, we can choose to be as responsible as we wish with such knowledge, for the actions that will transform and redefine us.

Those of us who have sought to live responsibly among all our relatives may call this an obligation. Such well-intentioned ethics can grow from a perspective of humans as the managers of the living world, or more amicably, as its stewards and custodians. This is a misapprehension, an environmental version of the 19th century's "white man's burden," one that will be used in much the same way, though Western imperialism has now extended its migration through circuits, gene sequences and molecular engineering. Indeed, you can already see expressions of this in the beneficently acclaimed green energy solutions centering around the biomass euphemism.

We have never been the managers we presumed to be nor ever will, ethically enlightened or not; nor are we the custodial shepherds guarding all our relatives. Our relatives need less of us in ways we might imagine and more of us in ways we do not. What roles we might envision bear the imperial seal. Our authentic, native place in the living world, among all our relatives, comes as we arrive, not before.

We are worried to find ourselves in the crossroads, vulnerable and uncertain any longer of

our place in a civilized world grown so indiscriminate and indifferent, so homogeneous that
there is little to distinguish it from nothing at all.
At a different juncture, Gandhi said we must be
the change we wish to see in the world. Yet such
change now arises from no position or role, but
through immense and diverse relationships negotiated, to our welcomed place among equals in
the living world.

Negotiating

A CIVILIZATION IS BY NATURE AND DEFINITION A centralizing impetus, drawing to its axes the resources, sources of energy available across the peripheries of its domain. No civilization is an exercise in local self-subsistence, but in expansion, an outsourcing of subsistence, freeing the center to accumulate wealth. The resource flow feeding this expansion is constantly moving past and through us: natural resources extracted and harvested, goods produced, services performed, labor bought and sold, the insouciant consensus of culture returned through the channels and forms of power.

The scale and efficiency of the flows, this conveyance of energy sources, for any timeplace, increases to the degree those resources can be made homogeneous, can be more collectively captured, uncovering the categorical, a singularity in diversity. As always, language betrays us, is our visage: energy, resources, goods, services, labor, production, consumption, capital, profit; each word and concept a package chosen for greatest scope of application and utility.

These words and so many others like them are conduits through which stream all that they may gather. We think them rational concepts, reasonably formed, sterilized to utility by some science of our making. This is not so. All the energy sources streaming past, aspects of the living world as are we, all flow to an event horizon not to be seen again in our lifetime or many others. This is no accident, no unintended side effect reflecting in part as an extinction event of planetary species, the sixth or Holocene extinction. We must see what is, we must see the act and call it by name. These are tools of genocide, terms of war.

Civilization does not negotiate for its subsistence. In the globalizing incarnation of Western civilization, this genocidal war of attrition became planetary in scope. This war will not stop, indeed cannot, until all available energy sources are exhausted. We can choose. Although we are a functional part of it, we remain of this civilization by choice and we can turn away. The civilization itself cannot.

Where would it go? Retire to a gated senior civilization's community in Costa Rica? Those few among us vested in its power centers know this with a certainty, and perpetuate the story of the good citizen, those who know and do what is necessary and reap the rewards.

We must negotiate, not with civilization, but with the living world, recovering our place among all our relatives. This is living by negotiation, not a thing done once, but a constant renewal of understanding. What this means, what we must do, a very many rather less civilized folks have been saying for quite some time. We have to loosen the fixed concepts civilization has imprinted into thought and language, learn and sense that all in and around us, animate and inanimate, is the living world and that we are intimately, inextricably joined and related. We have to learn to speak with these others, our relatives, and ask their permission for the use of their life, ask the earth for its stone, the water for its sustenance, the air for its breath, the sun for its heat and light. We have to ask in a language not our own and offer something of our own in return, for we are needed too, negotiating in good faith, in right relationship. And we have to listen and abide, most beloved, as a child does, with or without any answer we may recognize, until the voices of the others grow in us.

Voices

THERE'S A SINGULARITY THAT STALKS US, WHAT-
ever our collective, seeded in the unifying, limbed
in the gathering, that rides the semantic ridges
to direct chorus to one voice (herein the dan-
ger) that sounds something like us. The similar-
ity we recognize, the sameness nascent in unity
is vulnerable to the categorical color-coding that
grows in the centralizing impetus of civilization,
an organism that can by nature catalyze meaning
only in broad, simplified channels. Our common
strength, what animates and sustains community in the living world, is our immense diversity,
yet unless we treasure its many voices and many

hands above all else, we lapse into the vast mono-cultural channels.

Community is a local complement, emerging uniquely from the distinctive features it embodies. Without the expressive presence of all its members, human and non-human, it's a creature of the civilization, a hybrid that distributes and transports well, hence the plague of homogeneous communities. True community is exquisitely slow to find its tenor, to shape its focus, a child rapt in its sensing body. This is its resilient and endangered source.

Our civil monoculturating filter leads us to see first a profusion of objects and entities. This civilization is visually-dependent, a literate reflection, the sole subject to all objects. We see what we understand. Our ability to resolve varied points of view is limited by this line of sight objectivity. Unable to participate any longer in the solutions, we must solve and resolve the plenitude before us, rather than allowing this diversity to settle to its moment and gathered form, resolve's long inert etymology.

It takes patience. We are tuned to objects, not relationships, to results, not process. Strung from infinitely branching relationships, process makes it difficult to find a sequence that leads to verifiable results, to an objective answer we can wield. So we predetermine a result, make a map and tell it where we are and where we want to go. We isolate and simplify the routes, the relationships on which we hang process, the how of our intent. We are impatient and driven, progress waits for no one. We are the change our civilization has envisioned.

Although civilization is always centralizing, multiplexing diversity to mono-channels, its singular voice, something is happening. We're hearing other voices. Despite the central impulse, we've always been a multiplicity, a biotic community in the living world, in constant communication with all our relatives. We've simply not been listening. Fashioning civilization's element, the created world, we weren't paying attention. Told for centuries that we are alone, each of us a self that is our private property, we were self-absorbed. Presented with evidence and expert testimony, we believed that a fact could exist outside of the community of its telling, that what we told were no longer stories.

Community is our local complement, the voices of our shared place rising contrapuntal, a syncopated chatter and clap, wave and roll, flung call and response in endless cycles. As we are predisposed to think of it, not the sound of unity, of agreement. Wait, be patient, most beloved, this is us. It will settle. We've many voices.

Mono et Mono

IT'S BEEN A LONG TIME SINCE ONE AND ONE equaled two. There was a divergence, a time and place when measurement became an abstract equation: a difference between one autonomous unit and another...a binary distinction, an unrelated pair. Every additional occurrence of one unit is simply another unary factor, a sequence. Identifying when this divergence occurred is difficult, but it's notable the measurement of time, which clocked in to Western civilization near the end of the 13th century, achieved a prominence unequaled in civilizations before or since. Mathematics, founded on numeracy, does a utilitarian bit of handwaving to provide an ephemeral unit, a concept of number, functionally recurrent, yet nonexistent in the living world. This isn't a problem for mathematicians, who are used to such things. It becomes a problem when a civilization enshrines in its mythos a unary basis, a recurrent singularity expressed in time and space, expressing only quantity, mono et mono ad infinitum.

The mono familiars (monoculture, monopoly, monotheism, mono-etcetera) are what has grown from this seed, a dense fruiting of clones. We are drawn to such prolific singularity, believing it to be abundance, believing it to be wealth. Grown on the tree of this civilization, embodying and fulfilling its need through its monotypes, we distill to suitable containers the infinitely diverse streams of the living world. This is the purpose of our citizenry.

The flush of profusion in a successful monoculture is brief and poor sustenance. Look to the living world. Growth and regeneration thrives at the boundaries, the edges that define a collection of relationships, an ecosystem, a community. This civilization converges boundaries and edges, reducing all to its singular needs, an impulse inimical to its own health and survival. What stories do we tell ourselves of our gratifying progress? It defies reason though not power, not profit.

It's been a long time since one and one was a duality, most beloved, rich in relations, every single increase qualitative, a profusion of edges and boundaries shared and uniquely defining. It's been a long time since the living world came to us whole, in its full measure. Tell us, tell it again so we'll remember, so we can return to our place among all our relatives.

Languages

LANGUAGE IS A CHILD. ACADEMICS ONCE PRO-
nounced it an immaculate conception, but you've
only to roll a few syllables around the block to
know better. Communion, ritually usurped by
the ritual usurpers, conceives a language in the
relationship that is the gift of the other. Residing
with none, reciprocated by all who choose, this
gift arises from the commons so full of intent it
fissures, springs a call and a response, language
the child.

Civilization would claim this child its own.
Early on, the civilizers placed it with its clerics
for safekeeping, allowing it out only to celebrate
the rites convivial to civil power. Welcome ev-

erywhere, like air and water, it was too potent a child to be allowed to wander. The clerics made figures to harness it, arcane icons to entomb its mysteries behind their walls. 'Course, even in this much reduced state, language engulfed its keepers, spreading vines and veins that cracked and heaved the walls, wreathed the reliquaries, and joined itself whole in the wide arms of its inheritance.

The civil authorities were increasingly at odds. While the patriarchy labored at domestication, large-scale Tinkertoy constructs, logical siege devices, and machinations of language itself, the matriarchy fed the growing child, hung out with all the relatives and practiced lyrical biodiversity. The patriarchy's secular philosophy and commerce cleared pathways, connected empiric points, and monocultured meadows. The matriarchal lore rode scents and seedwings down rivulets and winds, across a geographical bloom of botanical and biological fecundity. The civilizers took measure of the complementary inclinations, and found the patriarchy to be more amenable to the centralizing aggregates of power. They shooed the clerics back to their catechisms, replacing them with ambitious young science, and benched the matriarchy in suitably domesticated institutions, making of the recalcitrants the original campfire girls.

Language now sat up straightly deterministic, near-strangled by grammatical neckties, and marched about in clearly punctuated white folk time to a calculus of rhetoric. The relatives didn't know what to make of it. The black hats, scientific civilizers, had proclaimed consciousness and intelligence human, as if that made any sense at all, and the child its offspring.

It didn't last long, of course. That kind of thing never does. The child once again outgrew its keepers. In time, the civilizers found their recourse in singularity (in this case, monolingual), and began a program to remove all the first born, a linguacide the civilization has effected in every locality it has entered. Like the offspring of every relationship in the living world, language is a living child, and as the immense diversity of this biosphere is reduced to monoculture, driven to extinction, it vanishes with the rest.

A community is highly localized, grown from the living world more abundant and diverse than we may know, humans never its author nor majority. Communion, sharing the embodied community, occurs with our every breath, our every act the telling of ourselves into the commons, all speaking at once unless we listen. Then we hear its time, most beloved, the metabolic call and response, and the language of the community is born, the child that can hold our true stories.

❧

Speaking with the World*

It's been a very long time, hundreds, thousands of years, so enamored were we of our aboutness, of how we could speak about the living world as though we were ourselves no longer a part of it, as though it, the itness, was there to be acted upon. An opportunity of a lifetime, if not ours then any one of our relatives. Every communing self aware and sensed at each other, no different than any other moment, any other day. Yet we could make it different, could and can make the day different, because the living world is the shape-shifter, and can be different. We can be exactly as different. How extraordinary and how common! We can speak about this, about our difference, about that sameness, or we can speak with this, a participant in an ancient conversation, with this not-aboutness, with this speaking, with the world.

We forgot perhaps, that all of our empirical understanding, our evidence about the world describes only what we are about and what is about us, which as fascinating and often wondrous as that may be, has a lifespan of "us," a cultural collective that every once in a while, for reasons unknown, longs for a broader scope, something a bit more universal, engagingly immortal. We were told, let's be clear, that we had embarked irrevocably upon our progress through time- space, whether upon an entirely evolutionary ladder or upon an exquisitely planned designer highway, and that we are under way all, no turning back now. Disembarking is of course impossible, except at designated stops, which oddly can be designated only after they have occurred. We forgot, forgot or were not told as children when we were being told, and now for reason's sake shall not be told, how immense is our power, that of all the living world, to choose and become.

Someday, most beloved, we will say with the world that it has been a very long time since we spoke about this. We will say there is so much that can be said about the world that to do so will empty the lifetimes of all of our generations unmeasured into us, into us as treasured stories that tell our people, what people we are, into being, into this our living conversation.

---

*Thanks to Robert Bringhurst and Gary Snyder.

Learning to Read

THERE'S A TRANSFORMING SEQUENCE WE MUST follow, a telling that wears its contours up winding steps, rising to precipices and rounded hills, down runnels into valleys and plains. There's a changing geography we must satisfy with our attentive passage, with the touch of our presence. There's a persistence, a distinct nudge of recurrent shapes that form in us their asking...is it their asking or ours?...that weave in and about us a pattern to recognition, to understanding. We thoughtfully oblige and thread to our home, to our loved places, the shapes as shown us, in their fitting sequence, their wondrous pattern; carry the tale as told us to hold open in our hand for our children, our people: the wings we found, the clouds, the seas, lands we have read.

The living world unrepresented by any explanations we make of it, of the parts we gather and assemble to a favored syntax, scribes its languages from its own elemental glyphs into sequences expanding and contracting in unique patterns.

Its expressions, all of us, coalesce or migrate in currents to our scope, periodic or aperiodic, all writ among relations across a metabolic time to cloud and disperse...what was said.

What was said when there was a meadow to hold you into the sky? What was said when the river bore past us to the sea its massive shoals? What was said when the mountain slid away crushing all in its departure? What was said when the fog filled the redwoods, when the snow silenced the woods, when the wind quivered shadows from barren corn stalks, when the brittle cold water tasted of limestone? What was said then?

What completeness we seek in thoughts of our own will not measure such reading, most beloved. If thought harbors intelligence, we must discover thought beyond our own, just as it is, and learn to read again.

Making a Place for the Story

WHEN WE THINK OR SPEAK OF STORIES, IT'S ALL content and meaning. We describe what the story is about, the measures of meaning that come to us. It's the words of the story, the images, sound, style, intent and impact conveyed by the content. As vital as the content of such a story is, to begin there is futile. We gravely underestimate the scope of the current story if we think we can tell its successor from its front porch, or from any place in its dominion. Any telling within these bounds is its telling, no matter how different or unique it may seem. The content of every story in this place is a renewal of the old story. How then could a new story be possible?

For the moment, forget the content. A story is much more than that anyway, though we've largely forgotten. The reason we no longer remember is a tribute to the efficacy of a literate upbringing. For us, a story is written, has content before we arrive to hear and know it. As any preliterate child can, in so many words tell us, this makes no sense at all. Our language developed to usefully intercede, to share and interpret our experience, in its evolution using an oral/aural medium, then some many millennia later, in a relatively few locations, a scribed/visual one. Our childhood memories are so vivid, so fully imprinted that we can very nearly be there again because they draw on our preliterate (and sometimes prelinguistic) capacity. Though we may think so, this ability isn't lost to us. It's still there under the overlay of our written world.

The story that we now live, and any story that can be lived, comes from a place that is content-free, a safe harbor, a place that opens to arrival and departure for the telling that needs to arise. In *extremis*, we've known this: those who have themselves or their loved ones lived through harrowing repression and known the necessity, as

Edwidge Danticat has it, of creating dangerously; those who have seen their people, language, their story, fading into a monotoned sea of civilization and are holding on; those knowing such loss that nothing remains beyond a breath and the turning day; those who walk away empty from a story that can no longer be theirs.

To make such a safe harbor, we need to look beyond what we can see, because all that we see, the entire created world, is the telling of the current story. A way to do this is to look with our other senses, learn the world again in the way we did as a child, before it was written. Since we've grown awkward and unfamiliar to our preliterate ways, it may be useful to attend to traditional cultures, folks who'd found a written language unnecessary, to learn more of what such a place might look like. It's interesting in this regard that early European accounts of indigenous peoples in the Americas regularly described these folks as child-like, and perhaps equally as interesting that we even now generally ascribe lesser intelligence to a child.

We are drawn to singularities, objects we can identify. Our language doesn't easily accommodate a concept that is neither an object, nor is differentiated as singular or plural. Yet this is what the story is; not an object, but a relation, a cultural analogue of undifferentiated embryonic tissue. It's expressed in any number of the possible shapes or ways available to the culture in its living community, the ungainly-termed "ecological community" from which the culture arises.

We tend to think stories are a passive reflection, and some may be so, but the presumption is a singularly literate one, finding an interstice between creator and created, a created word or shape filling an empty space or page. The story is as different in this respect as a carved puppet and the tree from which it was made. It is seeded by the culture-in-living-community, emerging among us not wholly our own, not wholly other, an epigenetic corollary. In us the story has metabolic life, birth and death. Among us it moves, exhibiting durations of ebb and flow, expansion and contraction. It is both conserving and adapting. Needfully metamorphic in seeking this balance, in its time the story reduces or amplifies particular aspects of the culture-community marriage that birthed and sustains it.

Like all in the living world, it's clear the story becomes itself in a particular time and place, developing bioregionally as we do, its locality distinctly ours, refined and tuned to the range and scope of our living community. Though we carry the story with us wherever we go, it's dependent on place in ways we aren't. In this regard, the animus of the story is more plant than animal, more element than plant, deeply rooted in geomorphology. We can, in time, reach an indigenous accord with the new places that adopt us; the story cannot. In the absence of the wedded living community, it fades to fossil, to precepts plugged into cultural life-support systems.

It has ever been that the story exists only in the community commons, and cannot be claimed by any person. It tells itself among all members of the living community, yet it's not the story's belonging to a community that is told, but a community's belonging to the story, remembered when it's remembered, lost when it's lost. This is why traditional cultures treasured their stories above all else. Who will tell them, who will tell The People into this world, when their story is gone.

The story has precedent, but is undefined, arriving never before but with us, at each telling renewing itself. This doesn't mean the story can't find expression in writing or any other medium. Yet, no matter how often or how widely the story occurs, it assumes shape only as it emerges among us, with us, at the moment of its telling, requiring in some way our participation in its shaping.

It's an old paradox that something so important could be useless, but this is so. Such a thing as the story can be purposed to nothing beyond itself, is useless by any measure or intent other than that of its own expression. It's not a result or product of empirical inquiry, nor of belief. No other character beyond that of its utter uselessness can sustain its creation. This, it turns out, is the source of its great power.

And this is the way a new story can arrive, most beloved, likely has always done so. One example of how we're told it worked in the past, is the way Raven did it when stealing light, ostensibly for himself alone, but effectively for the entire world. Raven's methods in this ancient story, shared among indigenous folk of the Pacific Northwest, are something like this: The living world, Raven's world, is without light, and he learns there's another place where the light lives. Raven travels to that place and uses whatever capabilities he has to become recognized by the keeper (all places have keepers) as a trusted part of that world. Raven patiently convinces the keeper to reveal the light, then quickly steals it, carrying it into the dark-enshrouded world from whence he came. Once in the darkly living world, whether by any intent or accident on Raven's part, the light assumes its own power and place among all.

Raven is a trickster, an instigator of disturbance, the results of his actions uncertain to both others and himself. Yet he is part of the living world, and as such, its representative, both because of and despite his self-interest. There are other elementals besides Raven, other ways the story can come into being, but the story itself lives elsewhere, and for it to live here, it first must have here the appropriate needs and means to become whatever it must be. Then finally, when our elemental need is clear, one of us will simply go retrieve it whole and bring it back. Oddly

enough, that's about as far as the ancient plan-
ning committees ever got. The journeys that followed were, like Raven's we're told, memorable.

What Grows from Here

WHAT GROWS FROM HERE COMES WITH ITS OWN energy, its own and that of its place, the ancestral start given, the potent burst that opens all doors and windows, that joins into place, into the sustaining relationships what grows from here. No need of coal, oil, or gas. No need of dams and powerlines or fleets of transports. What grows from here is what can, what fits, its ways reflected in the health of all the relatives, our community.

Lightly held and wielded, the work that grows from here feeds here. Farmers, ranchers, gardeners, orchardists, loggers learn to feed the soil. Fisheries learn to feed the streams, rivers and seas. All of us in the living world feed the air and the great transformations to heat. This work must fit to here, across many generations, its relationships rightly honored, closely attended, capably flexing and changing in the living accord, moved by touch most carefully.

The children that grow from here move and speak its language, breathe the breath of its plants and trees, ingest, host and enact its life. Children ours and with a belonging beyond us, among those of all our relatives, as all children of this momentous bioregion, this timeplace, restore and fulfill agreements in the larger living world. We show them what our people have become, the way we have come, how this place speaks and moves us, telling the story that carries us to them.

The people who have become themselves, distinct among all others in joining to this place, have grown from here into our recognition, into the recognition of all our relatives, as us, ourselves, The People. We are salted and scented by lifetimes walked on this soil and stone, by great trees opening to our hand, by vibrant plants drawn to nourish and heal, by the shared heat of blood fleshed into its element, by the gifts of our relatives. We are known and thereby honored in keeping the way, becoming in our time what grows from here.

What grows from here is held in place by all its relatives, the affinity gravity would express. Every plant and animal, every organism, stone and mineral, every element here is necessary, its authentic knowledge and use fulfilled here in its orbit. None of these, none of us can grow from here without all of us. Only then are we entire, most beloved, a whole expression, a word spoken only here, a step on which we also walk, a tier on which others depend and we so become, to horizons larger and smaller, what grows from here.

Wilderness

OUR HOME AWAY FROM HOME HAS ALWAYS BEEN
the wilderness, the place of our wandering when
civilization presumes a life of its own, its indifferent weight borne more closely upon us as it grows.
In wilderness, we step more equably, more carefully, known there since time began and knowing
we have there only what's given. The wilderness
always takes us back, reminding us we'd never
left, only cast to orbit round a civilized perch, one
more Freudian than Ptolemaic.

We always know where it is. After all, our
evolving genome is memory itself, wilderness
grown with us, cell to bone, song to science. Four
hundred years of our depredations in the Ameri-

cas left the scent of extinction in our industrious air, enough that we reserved places for the survival of indigenous wilderness. To the globalizing rationalist, there is a fundamental distinction between mind and nature, human and nonhuman. Accordingly, whatever indigenous wilderness was, it was not us. So indigenous people, wilderness embodied, were separated from nonhuman nature, severed as thoroughly as could be rationally conceived from their belonging; from their language, so they could no longer speak with all their relatives, and from their practices, so they could no longer act to become themselves. Nonhuman nature was parked empathically out of the way and displayed, with somewhat less empathy, in zoological confinement. This legacy has come from a mythos that denies the primacy of wilderness, our belonging, denies us our traditional refuge, a mythos now globalized in its reach.

We are on both sides of any wall, any distinction we construct. It's not that wilderness hasn't survived in its designated isolation, it certainly has. The long struggle of preservation, of conservation, hasn't failed, nor can it succeed in its historical intent. We protect it from ourselves if we can, but we protect only the expression we can recognize, the wilderness without us. Wilderness will never be designate, nor will we be its savior. It is and has always been ours. What we act to protect and conserve is a fundamental relationship, immeasurable in its extent, fearsome in its intimacy. We are known to it in process, in blooded heat, feeding light, swallowed darkness, in bone and soil, water to stone, wing to song. All that we are and do answers to its voice. We can go to it and we can call it to us.

We can call to us only indigenous wilderness, what grows from our belonging among all our relatives, our authentic community. It can be called only in its own language, from its own story, most beloved. This nativity, this language is shaped in its locus, its care in community ways. From the gift of its telling we'll hear the wilderness answer. This is a practice and it will come to us, again.

Successions

WE ARRIVE INTO THE PLACE OF ANOTHER, THE vestigial other, as does all life, arrive under our progenitors' impulse into an inheritance that is never ours but the gifts of the other, of all our relatives held in common, in trust; arrive, our senses unwombed, opening before knowledge all at once, pioneers in a place that is itself as alive as ever we will be, a place in motion, rolling upon the ebb and flow of others, other places, other times, passed along in metabolic language, to our succession.

Perhaps we are a consequence of all that came before us, yet it's only through our choice of scale and scope, as we'd envision it, that direction and progress appear, that we discover linear certainties. Change the scale, swing the metabolic axis, and different geometries apply, looped, circling, cycling, where direction, progression, succession as we know it, resolve to nothing more than our intent, swimmers in a river we'd not noticed. This is the living world, at any scope or scale another visage, an other, in a shifting dynamic.

Circling then, but what are we circling and what impulse moves us? Scoped to our planetary body, there is an apparent resolution to both parts of the question in light (electromagnetic radiation) and heat, its resonance in the living world. So far, this resolution seems to scale across all ranges, from the planetary to the molecular. New arrivals to an ecosystem, whether through birth, collective immigration, or iconoclastic wandering, cycle faster, spin through their transformative work of acquiring and engendering mass, fueling and radiating heat, reflecting light, coiling and releasing electromagnetic pulse, all at much higher rate than the old timers. Those elders, their communities, move in larger cycles at slower rates of exchange, in long established relationships refining these same transformations to a broader, more durable sustenance. Light and heat then is a resolution of our orbit and cycle, and gravity its universal pinion, its relation (bearing a profound resemblance to affinity) among all so embodied.

Yet these entities, new and old, reflect patterns of metabolism and timeplace, perspectives fitted to our capabilities, our needs. There are others, endless others cycling beyond our scope that bring aperiodic disturbance to any reliance on pattern. To expand our scope and scale, we craft ways to extend and amplify our biotic reach and vision, these technologies prostheses to our senses, successions to our indigenous means. Such an expansion requires fuel, our civilizing culture gathering to its core the heat and mass that is the product of our life, our consumption. The rate of this exchange is a currency, a moneyed transfer of energy from periphery to center. The periphery expands as available resources and our consummate capacity allows. Here is direction, progress, expansion: a patriarchy's blow-up doll inamorata.

We discovered early that it's a place's, a community's, first succession phase that is most productive for our needs, and we've learned how to keep a community in this state. Bound to its new arrival phase, the community performs its transformations at a high rate, creating more heat and mass to transfer along the established channels. Resources, anything that can be consumed, all others and ourselves, are exhausted at a higher rate as well, entering depletion stages that draw on much larger relationships. Because the community is held in first succession, the relationships that enable the consumption of its waste, anything the community cannot transform to civilized use, dissipate, and waste accumulates, also at higher rates. Only further expansion of first succession communities can sustain such a civilization.

We believe we now live longer and better than ever before, that we've amassed more energy and wealth than any prior civilization. We have the data. We can prove it. We've succeeded.

There's the parade, most beloved, our relatives dead and dying.

Perennial Life

THOUGH INCONCEIVABLE, AND PERHAPS FOR this reason alone, we presume infinity in all we do. Evolution, eternal life, the foundations of mathematics, the future, advances in technology, economic growth, our very concept of development...all as we know them, pull infinity out of a hat. A characteristic of our time, our civilization, yet wholly without basis in evidence current or historical. We have a faithful capacity for infinity that progressively impoverishes us and all around us.

The myth of The Garden, long misinterpreted, is a telling of a timeplace where all was in abundance, without distinction of self and other, knowledge and ignorance, cause and effect. This was a timeplace not eternal and unchanging, but seasonally blessed, perennially renewed by those who lived there, by the cycles of their days, the rise and fall of their lives and deaths. What knowledge came to this archetypal humanity, this male and female, was from a choice of sustenance. This was humanity's agrarian birth, when we assumed control of our food, thereby responsible for its place in the earth, for the labor of its production. A choosing of food's domestication, its husbandry, the annual rites of the soil, planting, harvest and storage. We fell upon the earth, to a station and place of annual accounts, lost to the perennial life of hunt and gather, gleaning what we needed from all around, from all our relatives.

There are gardens we do not see, nearly indistinguishable from all around them, yet bearing perennially a wealth of local energy. We may not have planted them, although having learned from the destitution we've visited upon the earth through millennia of annual tillage and seeding, and from the traditional gardening practices of some indigenous peoples, we now know how. We call them forest gardens, due not to their location, but to their multistoried nature, the plantings thriving by height (proximity to light) and companionship, of a size and scale befitting the ecosystem, the lowest story always the living soil.

There are plants we don't find distinctive, that produce inadequately, too slowly, or too irregularly to our measure, yet that do so perennially. Rather than chasing the dragon of infinitely greater annual yields, we could choose to coax sustainable offerings from neglected perennials. Because, grain fires the bellies of humanity, there are a few among us, like those at the Land Institute, breeding grains and doing this work. They know the annualized product of the living world has been receding for many years, along with the topsoil, the living soil, a thing we cannot create.

We cannot return to The Garden, nor to any other time, most beloved, but we can learn from our choices, the value as always of our stories, and found our communities on perennial life, thereby becoming so ourselves, an interesting and overlooked bit of congruence. Or we can continue the tried and not so true, faith-based annual acquisitions of technological or economic development. Choice begins in recognition.

Epoch

IT WAS GONE, THAT WHICH CALLED, BEFORE WE arrived, before we saw the place it once was, its imprints still in the soft earth, its scent in the fallen leaves. We were coming. How could they not know we were coming, that we never arrive alone, that many depend on us, were waiting too, for us to see, sense them, speak their names, help them in their passage and ours? How could such resonance, the living bound to us, be forsaken?

Some, they say, are made for another time and place, left to wander a lifetime without fulfilling the relationships meant to be theirs. A very old story told in many different ways, yet the map is not the territory, and the map the story gives us, its language, its mural played across this time, is a shadow of what is. In its dissolution, an epoch loses its own, and we are a river, spilling over the roads, carried now by current more instinct than memory.

Place and time are never parted. An epoch begotten energy, gene to generation, commons to community, what is made given into what is asked. So many ask only for more, poverty in any guise, borne into all received. Walk away from that breadline and you will hear what is asked of us, what was lost to us.

Bear fully the loss we have wondered to find, clear-brittle and ash-blown in the epoch's ending, seeded into what place we become, into the new.

❧

Nothing Is Written

IT'S HARD TO TURN DOWN SOMETHING THAT, BY its very name, advertises it won't cost you a thing, takes up very little space, and you can do anything you want with. It's long been called free will, appearing most often in uncertain times, and as it is with such notions, always in conjunction with its counterpart. (A porch somewhere in the middling of the multiverse.) "What are they on about?"

"It's a parade I think, on the subject of free will."

"Ah. Don't they know it doesn't make any difference?"

"Ssh, you'll hurt their feelings. They've done some very nice placards. Look at those diagrams."

"I like the cartoons."

Free will is good for all kinds of things presumably, and although we've been waiting for millennia for experts on the issue to give us the nod, it appears we still don't know whether we actually have any. 'Course, even if we do, just having the stuff doesn't mean you can actually use it, a consideration that has long kept clerics and barristers gainfully employed. Exercising free will turns out to be an education.

The whole question apparently arose when someone noticed they'd misplaced theirs, or possibly never had any to begin with, though the prospect sounded quite nice, and according to some leading authorities was indispensable really, hardly worth going on without, unless you were of the religious persuasion and had your free will circumcised to appropriate measure.

There are experts and hangers on who've perennially labored to reach virtual summits from whereupon they might have an unobstructed view of the issue. They've written and amassed stacks of evidence on the subject, which less generous souls have attributed to the uplift.

Some have looked determinedly at free will until their eyes bleared, have known its family for years and are able to trace its ancestry back to a few strands of DNA. They report that there's actually nothing free in there, and though nature has an incomparable playlist, it already knows all our favorites and which ones we'll pick next.

A convivial and equally determined group of colleagues applying utilitarian logic have followed its path to dichotomy, a binaried absolution, a prong of equivalence where either/or and true/false are its fundamental and lasting expressions.

Still others have uncovered the question pinioned between historical cause and effect, an a priori approach (less efficacious on origin) that attributes will's free appearance to the mirrored decorations of a common dementia, past causes and effects lost in a present flourish of the same.

Situated upon imposingly indeterminate summits are experts waving opposing flinty-edged proofs honed on unfortunate gods, clerics and kings, and asserting that free will quite literally blooms from the cells with which the beholder peers, how life asks itself the very question, rather than being assembled in conga lines of logic or DNA reflected under their esteemed colleagues lenses.

There are other points of view, of course. There's a lovely one that meanders between and across the virtual peaks and has been experiencing a considerate revival of late. It's all about dynamic relationships emerging into vastly diverse feedback loops filled with complex and subtle interactions, all the while expanding and contracting, back and forth, like breathing, or a porch swing.

"How do you stand on the question of free will then?"

"Quite gingerly, my son. Oh, I've had some kind of well up now and again, you know."

(Nods all 'round.)

"Do anything interesting?"

(Weighs the question with the squinty-eyed look that scatters squirrels from his bird feeder.) "Might have got me a woman."

"Careful now," said his woman of some years. (The porch swing picks up a bit of speed.)

Of course, all these perspectives are variations modeled across the spectrum of our unimpressive metabolic range, stories that we tell to interpret the immensities. Nothing is written. Though the literal figures pleasantly into our pages and thoughts, its auguries scribbled on the civil walls, it doesn't precede us. Those shapes ahead of us that we can never quite make out are a clouded exhalation, the breath of the living world as it speaks us.

"I was looking for something. It was fall. Smelled like persimmons, I remember. Head down in the trunk of the car and tossing things out. One was a tube of maroon paint. After a bit I heard a woman's voice: "Did you do that?" Looked up and there she was. Her eyes pointed me to the fence in the alley, where the paint tube had landed to great effect. "Might have," I said. "Do you like it?" She looked at the fence kind of critically, "Wants some lavender, I think." First time the Mrs. and I met.

"Which part of that was free will then?"

"Hard to say. Had that about it though, now I've come to know its absence."

Choices

OF ALL THAT WE HAVE LOST, HAVE ABANDONED in civilization's flourish and our own, never, despite what we may be told and may surmise, never has choice been taken from us nor ever can be. We can, to our peril, relinquish it to others, pretend it doesn't exist, or presume electing not to choose is not itself a choice. We may not find choices that appeal, but there in front of us, assuredly and without exception, they always are. In the usual meandering course of days, there is a vast field of them rising in our passage, flushed by the train of our intent.

When to us the great and diverse profusion of the living world resolves too quickly to definition, the choices grown few, and those on which we've arrived turn out to have been less than robust, grown now barren and infertile, it is yet our choice, called from our own intent that embodies the day, the next moment, here before us to be acknowledged.

What choices we recognize are distinguished by the values, the properties, of our fundamental relationships. To the degree that we know ourselves among all our relatives of the living world, our values are rooted there, expressions of the living world. When we know ourselves predominantly in the created world, our values are drawn from its expression, an extension of our time and culture, shaped by its dominions of power and wealth.

We choose a thing by our sense of it, rationality living comfortably among its peers. Empiricists protest that only rationale is verifiable, presuming as a constant the unverifiable objectivity necessary for such certification. We are to compile and assess evidence, review results, and deliver logicked conclusions to a demonstrably correct assessment. Then we may choose, our potential choices having circuited the established pathways. Protocols are useful, but necessarily limited to constructing their purpose. It's elementary then to be certain what that purpose is before committing ourselves to its outcome. The empirical protocol is purposed to the utilitarian, an encapsulation of our tool-making characteristic. Every outcome of this protocol is intended to be useful, to further the crafting, the technos, of the tool-user. In empiric hands, those of an empire, this utility is centralizing and translates into abuse of all others, the now dominant characteristic of our civilization.

Control is the apparent removal of choice. There are so many choices, we rarely recognize the displacement of a few, the forks in the road that go unnoticed as we focus on our absorbing destination. We most easily notice lack of quantity. Yet if the quantity of choices can be sustained, or particularly, increased, any qualitative differences can be disregarded, at least for a time. Essential poverty can then be obscured by a surfeit of advertised wealth.

There is no god before intent, preceding and succeeding generations of choice, yet manifest only and always in our choosing. Success or failure, what follows is always another, another choice. We balance on this razor edge, this crux. This is so for the entire living world, yet its choices are quite different from what ours have been (and include us, lest we forget), each choosing, a matter of life and death. The created world, product of a civilization, makes no choice, and no claim on us, that extends beyond its own sustenance. It has ever been that in right relationship, most beloved, our values align with those of the living world. This is no mystery, only a choosing to which we must attend.

The Gift of The Other

THERE'S ONLY ONE GIFT, ALL ELSE ITS SHAPE AND expression, all else the chemistry, the biology of its relations, of its substantial birth in the living world. There is only the gift of the other, not from our eyes, sensed as we sense, known as we know, never here when we arrive, but there, what we were, what we might become. Here, in this place it arises from the spring that twins us to no reflection or shadow, but simple truth, I and not I, always one and the other among all in the living world. If memory could follow, we'd know only the endless flood of our words and songs unheard, loves untouched, unseen. What was once a tree, a river, a son or daughter, mountain or bird, was once and may be no longer, we know all too well. We know the fragile husk of time, what becomes memory, what becomes solely because it cannot be followed. We know the loss of them, of them all, the sky that held their breath, the streams from which they drank, the earth from which they grew, on which they walked. We know the loss of the other, the only loss we will ever know, as we know its gift, the only gift we have.

Birth

THERE WERE SO MANY MORE THERE AT THE BE-
ginning than you might imagine. We hadn't re-
alized ourselves how many were carrying you to
us. The sea of ancestors, millennia of learning
encompassed and funneled to your moment. The
entire living world rising and falling to its death
and life, fusing in the centimeters of your geography, giving you its own breath, blood and bone.
All were there, most beloved, all, and we no longer knew the ways to welcome them and properly show our gratitude, the way the story is meant
to begin for each of us. So you arrived, ourselves
the only ones among our ancient relatives not as-
tounded at our ignorance.

Another incarnation of the living world, our given form and physiology becoming yours, opened to presence and absence, the yin-yang proto-relation of opposites. From your sensory call and response came the gift of the other, the metabolic gestalt from which all your relations emerge, the living page upon which all your stories are told. We heard you, were waiting for you, and the telling of the story that is you began, a story for some years we have told together.

This is difficult to say, because now we are speaking of a timeplace before language, and so this is where we must be careful and listen, rather than making of it something of ourselves. The proto-relation to which you called arose from your direct awareness in the living world, and from this came to you whole the telling of the living world itself, you among its expressions, and us, your people. Another relation, one that came to you slowly holds the telling of the created world, what we have made, the shaped and named geographies of the civilization.

The living world that gave you to us, is beyond our claim, retaining us in its knowing, and for this we have feared it, and as is our wont, attempted to diminish our fear.

The story that is you is bound to our relation to the created world, but it is a story, yours as much as you are its in the telling. Stories are infinitely mutable. If you wish, you can choose not to sustain the one that is currently you, and allow your life to begin telling a different one. The people of your story, your people, us, would rather you didn't know this, the utter simplicity of it. We've spent much of a lifetime creating this for you, and depend on this knowledge, the love from which we called you, and would not have you be otherwise. Yet, this is so.

The relation that bears your story and ours is vital to your people. We can admit of no other. This is the only relation that can continue the telling of our story. Without it we would cease to exist as a people. For this, we require your belief. We need you to believe there is no other relation from which your story, your life, may arise. We need you to believe there is no other people, no other life that calls to you.

Yet as long as the first relation, your relation to the living world, exists, you have a story unconstrained by any human construct. There are immense, perhaps infinite, relations emerging to us, with us, at every moment from the vast living world. There are other relations to which you can call, and which can call to you. Birth is one beginning. From our love we call you ours, but all of our relatives, all life has seen you, knows you.

Our people have lost the way and haven't the capacity to again find it. You know this. There are others like you. Go with this blessing, speak with your relatives, and become another story, another life, another people.

A Living

A FEW OF US ARRIVE TO ITS EMBRACE, BE-
queathed its cumulate favor, the valued properties fruited in one empire or another, its etymology factored in the industrious heat of many. Most
of us labor in its service, exchanging one precarious life for another, for dim passage to promise
of our own, those of our own. We have honored
it in name, the living we make, made of ourselves
and all bound to us, and all are bound to us. All
are devoted to our living, as are we to theirs.

We are more water than earth, more air than
water, shaped by affinities we can only guess, to
what purposes beyond those shared we story into
being. And beyond those shared, what can be our

purposed measure when air, water and earth are the elemental commons of the living world? What remains that is solely our own, our made living, our created world? What empiric data charts our rise among the elements?

The economy that moves us is not our own, its currency the stuff of life, wages only in kind. Trade in air, water, in minerals is an ongoing negotiation, carbon cheap. Exchanges move and flux more rapidly towards the local axis. Work and play, nearly indistinguishable, are constant, though of great variety and often effortless. Each moment critical, each choice perilous, each life, each thing unique. It is an economy of energy, movement, transformation, always seeking its level, endlessly molding every shape imaginable and unimaginable.

We have a living unmediated by human agency, without profit, a living that can't be made. Here among us is its practice, its knowledge. What shall we do for such a living, its living?

Good Work

WHAT WE DO SHAPES US TO ITS WORK, ITS IN-
tent, movement and object tooling us to its use.
Hammer, logic, keyboard, machine, performing
in our theatre, on our scaffold. The things of this
world don't begin or end at our thought, our fin-
gertips. No object creates nor is created alone,
but all participating.

What we do is done through and to us, that
which we share and are a share of, and though
we ennoble it upon our decision, the work is never completed, but carried into other lives, other
deaths.

What we see finds us in what we have done, shadowed into the past, the storied past that clothes our memory and the embodied past that feeds our breath. Finds us because what we can see also has its knowledge of us, for it could not admit our presence without its cognizance. Whether in infancy or ignorance, all find us in what we have done.

What we feel belongs without asking, un-asked into the hands, words, things held in what we do, so often indistinct. Always its shaping, this assemblage of feeling, this emoted property of other places, times, of others. Known then as it asks of us to become form in what we do, in what good work we have.

What we have become we've no need to speak of. Our work is telling, is always the telling of what good we can be for ourselves, our children, all our relatives in this living world. The intent it gives all of us is in our voice, in the timbre, the reasoned tempo of our rhetoric. Its movement carries us beyond any motion of our own, ebbs to a completion we may yet influence.

Look to the good work, most beloved, what

reward may be, resonant in its doing, and others will begin to remember how once this life was loved.

Practices

THERE ARE MANY AMONG US WHO KNOW SO much, who bring to us brilliance and wondrous accomplishments. We ask ourselves, our children, "What do you want to do? What do you want to be?" We ask, knowing the answers will change and settle into capable range, into varied intent, but we ask because we are asked, and in answering trace shadow puppets outside our windows, scenes in a floating world, illumined and colored by streams of promise, wistfulness, curiosity. We have accomplished so much, we say. We tell this history of a civilization or culture, of our family or ourselves, of our friends, this story of record, of results, the recognized products of our hard work, learning, and inspiration. We share the pictures, celebrate the events. Here we were in our hour. So should it be...unless we confuse celebration with attainment, unless we commerce only in achievement, and found our living on product and commodity.

There are many among us who know so little, who know nothing so much as our own foolishness, finding ourselves always at the beginning of a day, the ineluctable mystery of what comes next, and practice at this verge what learning may be. A practice done for its own sake is mutable and never completed. It grows by attending to the relationships within its scope rather than to the objects. Open-ended, adaptable, sustaining and easily shared, practices closely resemble the processes of an ecosystem, are likely ecosystem processes we express in human community.

A practice without end makes no sense to a culture of commodity. Why would we just practice? There's no product to distribute, nothing to sell. In a culture of practice, performance is a description, rather than a goal, the practice occurring in the commons, in public. We can make of such performance an event, a moment of record, gate the entrance and exact a fee...to what end? To honor and sustain the practice in our community, or to fund and sustain the enterprise of its performance? These are themselves practices chosen by a community, by a culture, and exist within a network of related practices.

A living practice ends when we cease to need it or are incapable of continuing. It also ends when we decide its continuance is its accomplishment, when the practice degenerates into dogma, rather than anima, when it's no longer sustaining, but sustained. It's institutionalized then, reduced to a model of its former self on cultural life-support, a semblance of what was and is no longer.

We ask ourselves, our children, "What do we do in right relationship? What sustains us among all our human and nonhuman relatives, our community?" We ask, knowing the answers will change and settle into capable range, into varied intent, but we ask because we are asked by the entire living world. So much is possible, most beloved, but not everything, and in this interstice we practice and learn.

Colophon

Letters from the Commons is set in Sabon,
designed by Jan Tschichold (1902–1974)
in 1967. It was created to work across
platforms: on both monotype and linotype
machines as well as handset type. The
roman is modeled on the designs of Claude
Garamond (1480–1561) and the italic on
those of Robert Grandjon (1513–1589). In
the digital age, this old style font continues
its tradition of clarity and grace on the page.

WARD STREET PRESS

Made in the USA
Columbia, SC
04 September 2020